MW00476745

BEAUTY, WONDER,

— and —

ᴛʜᴇ ᴍ MYSTICAL MIND

BEAUTY, WONDER,
and
THE MYSTICAL MIND

Wilson Van Dusen

CHRYSALIS BOOKS

West Chester, Pennsylvania

©1999 by Wilson Van Dusen

All rights reserved. No part of the publication may be reproduced or
transmitted in any form or by any means, electronic or mechanical,
including photocopying, recording, or any information storage or
retrieval system, without prior permission from the publisher.

Library of Congress Cataloging-in-Publication Data

Van Dusen, Wilson.
    Beauty, wonder, and the mystical mind / Wilson Van Dusen.
        p.   cm.
    Includes bibliographical references.
    ISBN 0-87785-388-6
    1. Mysticism.   I. Title.
BL625.V35   1999
291.4'22—dc21   99-32733
                                                              CIP

Cover art: *Brother Fox* by Richard Chalfont. Reproduced by permission
of artist and Nick M. and Jane Saitto. Full art shown on frontispiece.

Permissions: "Religion: A Human Enterprise" was first published in
Chrysalis IX, no. 1 (Spring 1994): 1–14; and is reprinted by permission.
            "Gazing at the Spiritual in an Icon" was first published as
"Spiritual Practice with an Icon," *Sacred Art Journal* 12, no. 1 (March
1991): 3–10; and is reprinted by permission.

Edited by Mary Lou Bertucci
Designed by Ox + Company, Haddon Heights, New Jersey
Set in Minion by Sans Serif, Inc., Saline, Michigan
Printed in the United States of America.

Chrysalis Books is an imprint of the Swedenborg Foundation, Inc.
For more information, contact:
Swedenborg Foundation Publishers
320 North Church Street
West Chester, PA 19380
or
http://www.swedenborg.com.

DEDICATED TO

ONE OF THE WORLD'S GREATEST

SPIRITUAL EXPLORERS,

EMANUEL SWEDENBORG, MY MENTOR,

EVEN THOUGH THE CENTURIES

HAVE TRIED TO SEPARATE US.

Contents

Beauty, Wonder, and the Mystical Mind

Chapter One

An Introduction to Mysticism

A MYSTIC IS SIMPLY ONE WHO has had the direct experience of God. Mysticism is a field of study that considers the experience of mystics. It is an odd field in some ways. Although the experience of God is everyone's potential, some feel it is impossible to achieve or the result of an over-active imagination. Several things are operating. There is widespread ignorance of the very nature of the experience of God, so it is unrecognized and under reported. The experience itself can vary from small incidents to life-changing visions in which a person loses all contact with this world for a time. Culture and religions vary widely in their emphasis on this experience. There is a general East–West division, with Eastern religions having centuries of experience in this area, while Western religions often doubt that the experience is even possible. So, it is as though most people need some basic training before they can even appreciate what is actually known of mysticism.

Because of my work, mystics come to see me. They often emphasize their one or two big experiences. I have to ask to learn of their little, present experiences, which are better indicators of their status as mystics. What of God is present here and now? If they have these little experiences, they are involved in an on-going life-changing process. The presence of little experiences any time is like a gem in one's hand, small but still beautiful and fascinating. The past big experience is more like a legend of a great diamond somewhere, elusive and unavailable. One is current; the other is history.

Mysticism is, to the surprise of some, a respected area in all religions. However, anyone can experience that God exists, whether or not that person is a member of an organized religion. My own definition of a mystic is a bit more demanding than that of the conventional field. To me, a mystic is really anyone whose life has been shaped by the experience of God. This is somewhat more than having a little experience. I call such people mature mystics. There are several indications of a mature mystic:

1. Their lives and understanding are an unfolding continuous relationship with God.
2. Mature mystics show *wisdom* in their lives, which means that they understand life itself rather than merely having a knowledge about particular things.
3. Mature mystics have had the experience of God so many times that they know how to find their way back to it.
4. Mature mystics have often experimented with various spiritual practices and have found one (or several) that is best for them.
5. Mature mystics, contrary to many people's expectations, come to support religious tradition, rather than rejecting established faiths.
6. Mature mystics are humble.
7. Mature mystics often have explored beyond their personal identity to the Universal Identity.

8. Mature mystics so love goodness that, no matter what their faith or religious tradition, they recognize this virtue in other people and in other faiths.

So you see here the true character of the mature mystic. Male or female, he or she is a person who has known God often. They are in the midst of an ongoing blossoming relationship with God, a relationship that is the core of their lives. Out of this relationship they grow in wisdom. They are humble; no one can see the All without feeling pretty small. No matter how sanctified their words, any display of egotism or vanity is a sure sign that this person is not a mystic.

Mature mystics may be adherents of any faith, but they tend to give their faith greater depth and meaning. Oddly enough, for this reason they are sometimes attacked by leaders of organized religions who may not distinguish a mystic from a heretic or a madman. Mystics tend to sense the universal, and this enables them to see goodness in other faiths. Mature mystics can sense the good so well that they tend to break out of the restraints of conventional habits. In this way they can be unusually creative in human affairs, which may go against the strictures of an organized religion.

How will the mature mystic appear? Will fire come out of his or her eyes and the air become alive with electricity when they enter a room? Not in the least. In Zen there are humorous stories of the great master who appeared to be so ordinary that he was disregarded. Mature mystics often seem quite ordinary. If they could perform miracles, they would generally avoid doing so. Needing to impress others is not part of the mystic way. However, acquaintance with them suggests quiet harmony. They are people of inner seriousness. They can come from any station in life, but there is some prevalence of mystics from the lowest stations. So, in the world of degrees and credentials, they might not appear to be much. There is a considerable tendency for them to educate themselves in the wisdom literature of their own tradition. After all, the experience of God is very pleasant, and sacred wisdom literature leads them back to this state. Mystics tend to gravitate to anything that even reminds them of this experience.

Some people seem almost determined to misunderstand mysticism. Rather than look at the broad definition of simply "persons who have known God," they accept alternative connotations that emphasize the obscure or occult. Because they don't want to be associated with the "occult," they proclaim that their leader was no mystic. I have encountered this reaction several times with followers of the teachings of the great mystic Emanuel Swedenborg. Anyone who knows Swedenborg should easily acknowledge that he was a mystic—that is, one who has known God. People who have not experienced God directly are often impaired in judging whether anyone else has.

Although some might narrowly contend that only people of a particular religion (*their* religion, of course!) can know God, this is simply not true. Here I will be speaking of a combination of contemporary mystics I have known personally and of the world's mystical literature. There are pagan, Christian, Jewish, Islamic, Buddhist, and Hindu mystics. I know of no religion that does not have at least some little signs of mysticism. Clearly, some religions do not promote the experience of God; but always, down on the individual level, some mystics turn up nevertheless. On the other hand, there are religions almost all of whose followers are mystics. Buddhism is a wonderful example. The whole of Buddhism is designed and intended to produce the experience of God. Buddhism is not really understood until it is seen as a religion whose main purpose is helping people to personally find God. Buddhism is a great storehouse of ways to God that have been tested for some twenty-six centuries. The greatest of these ways is meditation in which the mind is let go. Then deeper elements appear of themselves. Mysticism is perhaps like wildflowers. It manages to exist everywhere, but it flourishes best when cultivated.

Mystics range in age from infants to old people, people of all ages, with and without any religious education. I am an example.

My first major mystical experience, quite memorable even now seventy-five years later, was at the age of one in a crib.

I lay on my back in a crib. I later described the room so well that my mother recognized it. Sunlight streamed through a stained-glass window. I turned my head to stare at motes of dust rotation in the light and emitting rainbow colors. I entered a world of ecstatically beautiful experience. This was the first of a series of experiences in childhood.

In my professional life as a clinical psychologist, I have come to know of mystical experiences felt by criminals in solitary confinement, by the insane, and even by the most unremarkable person.

I recall one insane fellow singing while raking leaves on the grounds of a mental hospital. I caught these words: "There is no two. Reality is myself all through." This is a wonderful statement of nondualism. I also recall one criminal who had such a vision in solitary confinement that ministers would envy him. There was an African-American burglar who went quite mad and stared at the floor of a mental ward for days. Afterwards he told me that he had been shown a review of the lives of all suppressed peoples. Though he was now ready to help all minorities, his life just could not support his new ambition.

Whatever a person's background, the mystical experience is greatly enhanced through study under a mystic. A mystic friend of mine, Horand Gutfeldt, recently died. Horand was a Latvian who was forced to join the Nazis in World War II. He was wounded, captured, and interned in France. He encountered a holy, French Roman Catholic priest while in the prisoner-of-war camp. Horand, a Protestant, credits this priest as his real spiritual mentor. The priest knew that Horand was a Protestant Nazi. Yet, the men set religious differences aside. The priest said that he would teach Horand only if Horand agreed to always teach the truth. Horand agreed and entered on what was heavenly training in the midst of the carnage of war. He became a minister and remained a spiritual seeker his whole life. He died of cancer recently, but an incident sticks in my mind. From his sick bed, he said he would graduate out of this world in three days. He did.

The tradition of one person's teaching the way to another is so great that some people believe that all must have a guru in order to have enlightenment. But there have been great mystics without a guru, notably Jesus Christ and Buddha. Sometimes God is the guru.

With or without a guru, God is the ultimate master in this area. In the Eastern religions, it is said God acts through the guru. But basically the experience of God is everyone's potential. If you do not experience the Divine in this lifetime, you will when you die, as has been so well demonstrated in accounts of the near-death experience.

In some respects, religious training may make the experience of God less likely. The more controlling a religion, the less likelihood of its tolerating a mystical experience. Also it is common that religious officials cannot recognize the experience of God in another. Even though they are steeped in religious dogma, they do not know the experience of God because they have never had it. This is particularly true in Western religions, and far less true in the Eastern. One would think that religions would welcome mystics in their midst since the experience of God is supposed to be the core of all religion. But what has often happened is that religious authorities feel threatened by anyone who claims the experience, and not a few mystics have been killed or excommunicated from their religion because of their beliefs. Religious authorities, with no experience of God, cannot recognize it in others, and end up trying to destroy this most valuable seed of all. The Roman Catholic Church has, unfortunately, a well-documented history of condemning, excommunicating, or executing their great mystics. For example, Meister Eckhart, who is now proudly proclaimed as a great Catholic mystic, was excommunicated for heresy by the Church after he died. This seems presumptuous to me since, after he died, he was clearly in the hands of God. Why not let God decide his fate? Eckhart was one of Catholicism's very hard-working bishops, a man whose sermons were so gifted as to be well worth study centuries later.

Church authorities often get too caught up in the things of the world to be able to judge who has known God. I hereby make an offer to any church having trouble recognizing its own mystics. With the church's help, I will find its mystics, who then can act as an advisory board to the church. Then this board of indigenous mystics, steeped in their religious tradition, can advise that church on how to handle mystics. I have not heard of such hierarchical difficulty in Buddhism and Hinduism. Both carefully cultivate the experience of God and are likely to recognize and honor mystics. Indeed, Buddhist and Hindu mystics often become respected teachers. Mystics in the Eastern Orthodox Church, when recognized, often become bishops; after leading the church for a time, they often return to a quiet life in a monastery.

I mentioned earlier that a true mystic does not seek fame since he or she is a humble servant of God. However, some mystical leaders have felt the need to come forward and to enter the world's arena, even the world of politics. The great Mahatma Gandhi was such a leader. Though a genuine mystic, Gandhi's aim was to overcome injustice. He was shot by another Hindu who was unable to see the greater good for which Gandhi fought. In the moments of dying, he forgave the assassin and repeated, "*Rama,*" a religious mantra. In effect, in the moments of dying, Gandhi focused on God.[1] He was a rare mystic working in the political arena.

Except for Gandhi and Jewish prophets of the Bible, most mystics live quietly in harmony with their environment. Only a few write and set down what they have found. Lately, I have discovered a great Jewish mystic, Abraham Joshua Heschel.[2]

Heschel was a professor in a Jewish seminary. His writings trace Jewish themes to the very root of human experience. Over and over, he showed such wisdom that he had to be a mystic living

---

1. There are many books by and about Mohandas Gandhi, but I recommend *Gandhi the Man* by Eknath Easwaran (Petaluma, Calif.: Nilgiri Press, 1978) because it captures the spiritual aspect of his work.

2. Abraham Heschel, *Man is Not Alone* (New York: Noonday Press, 1951). Heschel has also written a two-volume study of Jewish mystics entitled *The Prophets* (New York: Harper & Row, 1962), which I also highly recommend.

with God for a long while. Like mystics in any religion, Heschel gave the Jewish way a new depth of meaning. It is a pleasure to walk with a true mystic of any tradition.

In my excitement on reading Heschel's book, I sent postcards to twenty friends who are also mystics. None of my twenty mystical friends is anyone of note. I enjoy a correspondence with mystics. Their letters are so spiritual and my answers are so carefully crafted that I have started keeping a file of them. It is a rare sort of correspondence. One Hindu friend has a *sadhana* or spiritual practice of surfing, so I wrote a poem on surfing the spiritual for him. I said that the mystical experience is mostly emotional, and he rejoined that it is largely intellectual. I, like traditional mystics such as Sufis, tend to emphasize the emotional. I do so to avoid the dangers of a presumptuous intellect that believes it can think its way into the presence of God. A cardinal truth in mysticism is that only God gives the experience of God. Yet I concede that there is some rational or intellectual quality in what is given. Mystics compare notes as do people in other fields.

The majority of mystics are identified with a particular church, so they describe their experience in the frame of reference of their church. There are a few mystics who are not identified with any church. I am one of these, and so is the little-known writer Lewis Fraley Gray.[3] My own experience has illuminated the universal. Indeed, I was in late adolescence before I even became aware that my experience was a part of religion. Having absolutely no religious training, and being raised in an atheistic or agnostic family, I simply did not know much of religion. When I finally discovered the variety of the world's religions, I felt that their strictures and dogmas seemed rather odd and lost. But the writings of all mystics, of all creeds, immediately spoke to me. Oddly enough, my younger sister, raised much like me, became a mature Zen Buddhist mystic. She is not given to many words or explanation.

---

3. Lewis Fraley Gray, *Speaks My Soul* (n.p.: Sparks, Nevada: 1994).

The last thing she will talk about is Zen Buddhism. She reacts to my mysticism as "too many words," and in a way she is correct.

Because I perceived the same heart in all of the mystical traditions, I learned to adapt to the various cultures involved. Through my reading in the works of Abraham Heschel, I am just coming to understand and appreciate the Jewish tradition, a religious form unlike any other. For me, as a mystic, each of the various traditions is speaking of the one God in its own way. I long ago came to appreciate that the One has countless names, so *Rama, Allah,* and *Elohim* sound as sweet to me. It is much like speaking a variety of languages. They are not so far apart since they all speak of human affairs. I can also appreciate that some only know God through their religious tradition and that they may reject all other traditions as somehow suspect. Still, it is good whenever any man or woman finds his or her own way in even one tradition. I, on the other hand, feel at home in all varieties of mystical experience. On my desk are a white porcelain statue of Quan Yin (God's compassion) and an Eastern Orthodox icon of St. Innocent of Irkutsk, while on the wall are a Buddhist mandala and a lovely Japanese print of a temple. All these are one voice to me. The different traditions are like varied plants in the garden. Do they not add to the overall effect, each by their uniqueness? Swedenborg wrote about heaven's becoming ever perfect as its numbers swell. Picture each spirit entering heaven with its own unique experiences, each contributing something new—it is this that contributes to the perfection of the whole. So, while I can appreciate those who can only understand mysticism from their own religious view, I am one with a natural love for mystics of all traditions.

Despite the varieties and levels of mystical experience, the concept of mysticism has been well documented and studied. Mysticism is a field. The true literature of mysticism is a little odd. There aren't many mature mystics who write their own accounts, so, for me, the contemporary literature is a little barren. The great mystics are well known, usually referred to in encyclopedias. Indeed, most of the great mystics are historical figures, such as the

Greek Plotinus and the Christian Pseudo-Dionysius. This history of mystics can also be found in the world's great religious texts, such as the Bible, the Hindu Upanishads, the Chinese Tao Te Ching, and the Eastern Orthodox Philokalia. All of this literature is ancient or fairly old. Swedenborg is a near-contemporary mystic, having lived in eighteenth-century Europe, and yet his writings are now over two centuries old. The Upanishads are nearly four thousand years old.

I should comment on the contemporary mystical literature. I buy many contemporary works that sound promising and often find them so shallow that I end up giving them away. There are some writers, however, who have studied mysticism and have contributed to an understanding of the field. Both William James and Evelyn Underhill—neither of whom claimed to be a mystic—showed such an exquisite understanding of and sensitivity to the experience that they have been voted in by the union of world mystics.[4] How could William James and Evelyn Underhill succeed so well when others fail? Very simply, they had a feeling for the subject. Mysticism is about one central aspect of reality, the Universal Oneness underlying all reality. Those who have known oneness tend to detect it in all things. Those clever about a thousand bits and pieces cannot really show us oneness. Most commentaries on mysticism are done by rather academic people who forever analyze how this one mystic is unlike that one. Such commentators seem to lack the experience of God and the sense of the underlying unity. They see the surface and endlessly analyze every difference they can find. A friend recently sent me a philosopher's analysis of the history of mysticism. The author tried to compare the great traditions. It was a thousand bits and pieces of differences. Not having had the experience, he couldn't find the underlying unity. Here was a clever intellect, but God was missing. I threw the book out.

---

4. William James, *The Varieties of Religious Experience* (New York: Modern Library, 1902); and Evelyn Underhill, *Practical Mysticism* (New York: Dutton, 1915). Underhill has also written the well-known work *Mysticism*, but I think of this particular work as overly academic.

On Returning from Mystis

As a known, dyed-in-the-wool mystic, I often receive items related to my field from various people. One friend, a mystic in her own right, recently sent me a history of mysticism. This particular book was pretty good; but, as I read it, I kept grumbling to myself, "No, this isn't the way it should be done." Though I sensed it was wrong to present the material thus, I could not see a better way to do it until I slept.

So, herewith follows my history of mysticism presented in such a way it should make sense to all with a simple analogy. Let us say there is a distant alien land called Mystis. Down through history, from time to time, a traveler finds his or her way to Mystis and comes back with a report of this fabulous land, which is widely read. Now, if you are a mystic and gather up all these reports of Mystis, suddenly, lo and behold, all the reports appear to be of just one place. And thereby they make sense. I have been to Mystis, hence my grumbling at a bits-and-pieces report.

Now there is a remarkable feature of reports of Mystis. The people who went there were of different times, cultures, religions, and languages. Because of their varied approaches and backgrounds, we could expect reports so different that we might well have trouble recognizing it as one land. And yet, to one who has been there, these different people are describing the same landscape. Take the Hindu Upanishads, created in an oral tradition in India of 2000 BCE. Yet its account of the highest aspect of Mystis has been assented to by other visitors to Mystis ever since. Christian and Muslim visitors come back with similar reports. In the 1700s, the European Emanuel Swedenborg resided in Mystis for decades. Though his reports contain amazing detail, clearly it is the same land.

There is also another central aspect to all of these visits to Mystis. A Christian, Buddhist, or Sufi visitor comes back somewhat changed. It is as though Mystis has such a universal aspect that those who return become citizens of the Universal. Though they may remain Christian or Buddhist, they now come to see their native traditions as aspects of the Universal. This is so characteristic an effect of a visit to Mystis that a love and understanding of the Universal underlying all our apparent differences become signs of having been to Mystis. Visitors are changed, just as those who have had the near-death experience are changed. It is hard to look on the Universal and not perceive it underlying everything. It would shock those who have not been to Mystis to say our religious differences look incidental from a viewpoint of the universal.

So, here is the whole history of mysticism with all its bits and pieces of complexity. Over the ages, many have managed to visit Mystis, some for longer times than others. It is a land of immense unity, and visitors come back as citizens of the Universal. I do not believe that such different people over the ages could visit any other country and come back with such a wide agreement. Nor would they come back as citizens of the Universal. To me, it remains astonishing that, by visiting Mystis, I have come to love the Upanishads, Plotinus, Swedenborg's writings, and all the other reports. It is so good to be reminded of the highest one has known. Yet, because each of these reports contains the Universal, any one of these texts, studied, reflected upon, and approached in love, can lead me or anyone back to Mystis. With this end in view, one path is quite as good as another. Our lives are so many varied paths to one end.

Please retain from this brief "history of mysticism" the sense of astonishment that so many over the ages have been to Mystis and carry back the Universal. Then, all these apparent religious differences will seem a part of a single fabric of an amazing design. You should go to Mystis, too. It's the trip of a lifetime in a double sense—the most memorable trip possible, but also, as it turns out, it is what life is all about.

Thus, a million bits and pieces of a history of mysticism are condensed into a single unity.

Chapter Two

The Experience of God

IN MOST DEFINITIONS OF THE
mystical experience, it is often said to be ineffable, that is, beyond words. This is partly true. Yet there is value in successive generations' trying to describe the experience better. This helps others to recognize the experience in themselves. There is no difficulty in recognizing the higher level since the Ultimate makes itself known beyond all doubt. It is the little, lower-level experiences that are critical because they are often not recognized. Recognition leads people to seek further. With repeated experiences, the individual eventually comes to realize that he or she is in the hands of an ultimate wisdom that is guiding the way.

There may not be any person in existence who has not known the lowest level of the presence of God. Most often, the earliest experiences are found in nature when we are simply free and relaxed and ready to enjoy the wonder of existence. In these early

QUESTION: HOW CAN ONE GIVE LEVELS TO OTHERS + TRULY SUBJECTIVE AND LEVELS OR VALUES CAN ONLY BE GIVEN BY THE PERSON EXPERIENCING.

experiences, we may feel a certain elevation of state, as though this natural setting, this time and place, has become perfect. In this state the boundaries of self-versus-world dissolve. Somehow, in the beauty of nature, we become a part of this perfect whole. We can linger in this enjoyment. There is no hurry. Such a pleasant and joyous state of quiet wonder may ever after be remembered as the ideal. This is the lowest level of the experience of God.

Think back for a moment on the natural experiences you have had. They could have occurred in a park—perhaps one as grand as Yosemite or as small as a community memorial park, even in a secluded garden. The experience could have come upon you as you gazed at mountains or at the ocean. The place will vary; it is whatever setting you allow your spirit to resonate with. There you felt a calmness and joy that relieved your spirit. For those moments, you felt renewed and knew that you could go on because there is this state to return to for comfort and renewal. It was a moment of *feeling* connected to what is.

Now let me step outside this common experience. If you are a religious person, the state may seem like God present. However, it is not diminished if you know of no God except the wonder and beauty of nature. I say this because, for some people any thought of religion or God may spoil their experience. The idea of God introduces an alien element they cannot recognize. Yet, without the "God" label, the transcendent moment in nature has all the marks of the mystical experience. The experience tends to overcome the isolation of a beset ego. The boundaries of me-versus-it fall.

As a child, I made up my first religious ritual in this state. I would stand like an ape before the wonder of the sunset every evening. At about the age of nine, I needed some sort of ceremony. I stood like an ape, both to recognize my own primitive ignorance and as though to identify with primitive man. The sunset was so impressive that I assumed that a primitive man would feel as I did. It seemed like an odd thing to do but quite appropriate at the same time. The ape stance has disappeared, but I still salute nature.

The feeling of unity between one's self and all of nature is the central element of the experience of God. Everything is One, which is a central theme in the Hindu Upanishads and in the writings of Swedenborg. All is a One, and the person is somehow an aware, appreciative center in this Oneness. This simple and common experience is a fitting introduction into the experience of God. It has all the elements. You feel elevated into a higher, more harmonious, and joyous experience than you usually have. You are introduced to Wonder. And somehow it, you, and everything are One.

There are even subtle connections to mysticism. Having found this state, can you then create it? Even if you go into the same natural setting, can you make the joy and sense of Oneness? Likely not. In effect, the more you try to fashion the experience your way, to fit your needs and expectations, the more you succeed in blocking it. For the experience of God consistently blossoms in leaving yourself free to experience what is around you. You become egoless. Trying to fashion what you conceive to be the proper state is the opposite to letting be. The more "I," the less wonder; the more "It," the more wonder. I know a woman who had a full mystical experience while in childbirth. She worked for a year to give birth again on the same day of the year. Of course, she failed. So, a key is in letting it all be and in enjoying the wonder around you. There is no egotistic way of creating wonder, but it is easy to find, if you let all that is present come alive and reveal itself. The experience of God can only be given by God. At best we can let ourselves be receptive. *GOD IS, ITS ALREADY GIVEN ITS THERE, HERE NOW*

Shortly I will try to describe a higher mystical experience. It is very much like that above, but it is deeper in its self-revelation. While "God" may be missing for some in the natural state described above, there is no escaping God in the higher mystical moment. But so many curious people ask at this point, "What does God look like?," that I will try to answer this question from the experience itself.

Most people who ask what God looks like are thinking of the

GOD IS ALWAYS IS: GOD CANNOT BE MISSING — GOD DOES NOT MISS — WE" MAY MISS...

ordinary perception of objects. I see a roll-top desk in front of me. It is there; I am here. I can appraise what it looks like and name it. This kind of simple object perception is not possible with God. At best you might visualize your concept of God, perhaps as a white-bearded old man. In another culture, a person might "see" the God he or she sees in the temple, perhaps as a blue-skinned Krishna or as a tranquil Buddha. But in the higher mystical experience, you disappear. It is as though the Divine totally overwhelms the little self. There is no little self left, no one left to look and judge. There is only God's life. A scientist of my acquaintance finds it hard to believe this state can occur. For him, all knowing comes through object perception. He forgets that we can know just by being, i.e., know humanness through being human, know love through loving. And we can know God by entering the life of God.

So let me try to answer in a deeper way what God "looks like." God looks like all there is simultaneously. God looks like infinite joy, wisdom, and understanding. "Yes, but in what form?," you persist. Why, the form of all forms, of course. "Yes, but what in relation to man?" Why, everything, of course. I hope you begin to sense God does not take on a form like any other object. To experience God in any particular form is, at best, a very limited perception. I would ask anyone who reported having seen God in a particular form what they *felt* in the presence of this "God." It may be that they are so form-minded they overlooked the central feeling of the experience. If they felt none of the elevating qualities— joy, wonder, beauty, peace, wisdom, the very nature of the Divine—then I would suspect they have deluded themselves or met the demonic.

And I should speak of the noetic because it is different from ordinary knowing. In ordinary knowing, the kind of knowing cherished by my scientific friend, there are I, my thoughts, and the world of things. I am like a little microcosm free to construe the world around me as I choose. In the experience of God, however, there is direct knowing. All the little apparatus of self is overwhelmed by an infinite knowing. The Divine manifests, delights in showing Itself, which fills the little vessel of self to overflowing. A group of ministers were surprised when I once said that I could far more easily doubt my own existence than doubt God's. In the noetic experience, there is no doubt. Later, in the ordinary world, doubt may return, although, after having several transcendent experiences, doubt seems foolish. Noetic knowing is knowing given in such plenitude that doubt is not possible. *Direct* knowing. It is even possible to know as quite certain something that the ordinary you cannot really understand. In fact, this is common in mystical experience. You are shown, and know in that sense, far more than you can understand. But, after all, this is true in ordinary life too. We are all human, but how well can we describe and understand all that is involved in being human? We know and yet don't really know what it is to be human.

There are degrees of the mystical experience stretching from momentary delights to the experience in nature described above to even greater experiences. The major experiences are likely to arise in someone who remembers and treasures the little experiences. Seeking God for some time also furthers the experiences. Part of this seeking may lead to finding spiritual practices that work for you. Swedenborg read the Bible as though God were present and would guide his understanding. I developed a practice of simply gazing at an icon for fifteen minutes or longer, a practice explained in a later chapter. Actually, my childhood ritual of gazing at the sunset was an early, and perhaps unconscious, venture into this area. Some sort of consistent practice speeds up progress. Remember that mysticism is like wildflowers. It can grow anywhere, but it does better with cultivation.

Can you solve personal problems this way? Yes, but with qualifications. The seeker can pray for the highest good that is needed. In my experiences in gazing at an icon, the answer has sometimes come immediately. But on other occasions, days of seeking passed before the answer opened up. I discovered that I could not really understand the answer until I was put through subtle internal preparation. Then, when I was prepared, the answer was apparent.

Indeed, quite often, after this process, I have found that the answer was higher than I expected. For instance, I was having a physical problem and sought guidance on how to deal with it. The answer was given: I was somehow to dwell on myself. But the answer was so universal that it applied to all forms of awareness everywhere. It was as though, in seeking an answer for me, I was shown something of cosmic scope, which can hardly be described here. This sort of experience has given me the delightful sense of being in the hands of a higher wisdom that knows precisely what I am and what needs to be done within me.

Sometimes in their enthusiasm, people will emphasize that their avatar has perfect enlightenment, after which all human problems cease. This is most often seen in Hinduism. I, however, believe the emphasis on perfect enlightenment does a disservice. First, perfect enlightenment will be the joyous destiny of only a few. The average person is far more likely to embark on an infinite progression of learning, through this life and even the life to come. Learning is infinite. The emphasis on perfect enlightenment singles out one or two persons, and makes the rest of us seem inadequate because the goal it sets is nearly impossible. The truth is that we are all on the Way (whether we know it yet or not), and we have all made progress. Attaining knowledge is not a competitive game with a winner and a lot of losers. Learning never ends, a fact for which we should all be thankful. For, after all, there is no hurry. If you are leaning, then you are on the Way.

Now let's return to the major mystical experience. As with the lesser experience in nature, the major experience opens when you feel very free in quiet reflection. It is as though time, as a flow of events, slows down. There is a growing sense of the eternal. The life in you expands into Life itself everywhere. At this point, a problem you long carried may open and be fully answered. There is a strong sense of Presence within and without, for they are the same. How to stay in this Wonder? Simply enjoy it. Swedenborg describes the spiritual as a bird of paradise that flutters so near your face that its wings touch your eye. The All becomes manifest;

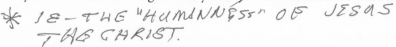
* IE — THE "HUMANNESS" OF JESUS
THE CHRIST.

indeed it is manifestation itself. There is just One Life. At higher levels, personal identity simply disappears; there is no I-versus-it. In the realm of the One, all dualities have passed; no duality is even possible. It is as though your personal identity and your awareness of this world gradually reassemble in time, leaving a stunned self. You were given more than you could contain or understand. The Lover has given to you "pressed down and flowing over." Some Sufis have complained that the fragile vessel of self may break. Let it break. It no longer matters. Ultimate love is given freely. There is nothing to fear. You are in the hands of loving Wisdom itself. The aura of the higher mystical experience can linger for days or even weeks, giving a heightened meaning to everything.

Remember the experience. Look for everything that reminds you of it. In some respects, mystics need the accounts of others because these may well give deeper understanding to their own mystical experience or to their own religious tradition. The words of other mystics can carry you back into the vicinity of wonder. Remember, and come back to the circumstances that recall the experience. Never fear that your love does not reach God. Love is spiritual communication itself; it easily communicates through all the worlds.

Afterwards, you will have met the lover in so many places and ways that it becomes apparent the lover is always there, waiting, most ready to show itself. It is the essence of life itself that lovers seek, and find in each other, even across time and through all circumstances.

We really are poor, blind, meager vessels. But even this vessel was created out of Wonder and contains Wonder. What ignorance or stubborn stupidity we must have to dodge the Ever-Present. Some fear death and do their best to cling to painted youth. Well, for heaven's sake, die and meet Wonder. From Wonder, you will wonder what kind of fool feared dying. As Plato said, die daily. Give up yourself every moment. The death of the self is the birth of all else. Die to live. Look at the near-death experience, which is a form of the mystical experience, for what happens when the body is given up.

You shouldn't worry about the loss of self. Those who find their way to Wonder then enter upon the greatest relationship. Wonder knows you so well and can be seen working through every circumstance of your life. Of course, Wonder will hurt you now and then. It is all part of your education. It reforms you in the midst of life. Yet, despite any occasional tribulations or setbacks, your life is the unfolding of a lovely design.

People who have enjoyed mystical experiences want to aid the design of creation. After all, since everything is One, they have become part of the design itself. They seek to be useful in life, to contribute something to the All. I feel that those who have found more have some obligation to aid others who are interested. This obligation is not onerous. It grows out of the joy of sharing, of breaking bread with friends. It does not matter, in the infinity of things, whether your contribution is big or little. In the midst of whatever you do is the love that communicates with the Whole. In being useful, in reaching beyond the self, lover comes back to Lover.

But why this whole trip from helpless infants to mature individuals, just to find the way back to the Design itself? Each of us is learning through his or her life. Returning to the Whole, our personal life's learning enriches the Whole. I mentioned earlier that Swedenborg says heaven becomes more perfect as it increases in number. He should know because he visited it for a long while. It is sufficient honor that a knowing little vessel becomes a part of the Whole, part of all there is.

I have sometimes been asked how I keep an interest in these experiences so long. Well, beside the fact that the experience itself is attractive, the experience of God is the key to everything else. Why are we created into life's ups and downs? What good is it? The experience of God opens up the entire design. It is the answer to everything. It is actually easy to understand how you can keep interested in the mystical if you've ever experienced it.

We humans are poor recipient vessels with limited powers. We can live our life for good or ill. If we live badly, we conceive of ourselves as independent units, cut off from everything else. If we live well, we find our salvation and highest joy in becoming an instrument of Wonder itself. The mystical experience shows the way to living well. It is a glimpse outside our limited puzzle-box selves to the wonderful design of the whole. Is it for everyone? Absolutely yes.

People tend to conceive of God as like themselves, as can be seen in the Christian conception of Christ, in the various human-like deities of Hinduism, and in the Buddha. Buddha is both a historic figure and a useful image of God. Swedenborg says we need the concept of the human to approach God, who is the Very Human. But for a moment, let me cast the whole drama of mystical experience in less anthropomorphic terms.

The mystical experience shows that the whole of creation is an integrated Wisdom—integrated because, at its highest, it is clearly One; Wisdom, because it makes existence a coordinated whole. The higher you go in levels of existence the more it reveals itself as infinitely wise. Notice that there is nothing in this description that suggests a *form*. If asked the form of this integrated Wisdom, I would respond that it is the form of all forms, a concept that, I hope, shatters any lesser ideas of form.

The next question to ask is what we are in relation to this integrated Wisdom. We are an aspect of it, an emanation of it. In no sense, except perhaps in our own fantasy, are we cut off from it. All our powers, however great or limited, are derived from its powers. We have an awareness only because it is Awareness itself. Its awareness stands behind ours and gives ours a semblance of independence and life.

We can examine the traditional religious idea of salvation from this frame of reference. We are, in some respects, condemned if we try to cut ourselves off from our natural heredity by conceiving of ourselves as detached and independent units. Salvation is achieved by coming to understand the real situation—that we are an aspect of this integrated Wisdom. Out of this understanding and acceptance, we come into some sort of role or function within the cosmic order; that is, we begin to function as a useful part of the interdependent Whole. This is the real Way for the individual, who is ultimately just a very limited functional aspect of the All.

This is what the mystical experience affirms and what the great mystics ultimately come to know. This is not to say the anthropomorphic image of human/God is wrong; rather, this conception is a useful step on the way, a step so many need that it must be respected. But as formulated above, as beyond form, Brahman is *netti netti*, not to be spoken of as limited in any way. The Jews were right not to try to say the name of the Ultimate. And this formulation is closer to the Buddhist Ultimate. It is beyond form, beyond any limited conception. Pseudo Dionysius was correct in saying we can approach the Divine best by saying it is not this and not that. But, wondrously enough, the mystical experience shows that the Divine is not beyond knowing by being. Why? Because it is the very heart of being. This is not as strange as it might first appear. Lovers can appreciate love, but a million volumes would not capture every aspect of love. And each lover would say even these million volumes did not capture *his or her* love. And this is true. We know awareness by being aware, humanness by being human. Knowing by being is the subtle, ever-present way. The Ultimate, being ever present, is particularly accessible this way.

Chapter Three

In Appreciation: A Poem

I WOULD HAVE SWORN I AM NO
poet. But then one day, in the midst of an intense spiritual experience, there suddenly emerged a style of blank verse. As with most of my mystical writing, I *felt* something about to emerge. In the midst of this experience, key phrases may come to me. I don't really sense the central theme and organization until it is all set down. Then the poem's theme and organization come as something of a surprise. It feels as though the poem has been given to me.

Of course, it is common for mystics to express some of their highest experiences in the form of poetry. In comparison, prose seems slowed down, static, and labored. In poetry, we can soar in brief phrasings full of implications. I am surprised how each nuance carries weight. I once had one of my poems printed with one word wrong, and for me it was destroyed. As with the ancients, I would consider singing and dancing or whatever else to express what is here.

This is an attempt in a literate form to convey, by implication, the quality of an experience. View it as a condensed essay.

IN APPRECIATION

*The ultimate aim of existence is,
oddly enough, simply the appreciation
of this moment.*

*This seems quite odd.
The Ultimate!
Must be Something Big!
But the appreciation
of this moment
is so little.
One must
be in appreciation,
to see It.*

*In appreciation
we are in harmony
with what is.
It is quite nice,
just as it is.*

*But more than that.
In appreciation
the moment speaks.
It is full
of silent portents.
Things stand friendly,*

alive,
gesturing to us.

But we can also
look at ourselves
in appreciation.
The things out there
are alive in me,
existing in my awareness.

The one in appreciation
is Awareness,
the meeting place
of all that is.
Standing in the Place,
the happy meeting place,
of Awareness.

And appreciation says,
"Ah, it is fine,
just like this.
It is sufficient
unto itself."
This moment
is the substance
of all moments.
So it doesn't
fire off rockets,
or make a big commotion.
Precisely its mystery,
that it is here,
and is quite sufficient
in itself.
That is its message.

Look,
just like this,
quite simple.
All there is,
here in this moment.
The image
of all images.
Quite primal.
Awareness
found Itself,
here in the simple present.
The little image
of all there is.

Surprise you?
Its peace,
satisfaction,
its littleness?
The Ultimate Aim
of the Whole of Creation
is in the appreciation
of this moment.
Amazing.

Chapter Four

Religion: A Human Enterprise[1]

I HAVE SPENT MOST OF MY LIFE in comparative religion and at various times have been identified with Buddhism, Roman Catholicism, Protestant sects, and most recently with the Eastern Orthodox Church. So, I feel qualified to present an overview of and say something illuminating about religion. But, as I originally conceived it, the topic proved exceedingly difficult. I could not stand above religions and take an overview without getting into what I consider the scandal of competing religions. It is as though religions have borrowed from advertising, and many assert that they are each the one, true, and best product. If this competition does not seem scandalous enough to you, then look at the buildings of Beirut (circa 1993). I recall one cease-fire

---

1. This essay was originally published in the journal *Chrysalis* IX, no. 1 (Spring 1994): 1–14. Slight editorial changes have been made. The theme of that volume was "The Future of Religion."

between the Moslems and Christians, in which nine were killed and sixty-five injured in one day. Over and over as I approached my attempt at an overview, I kept running into internal issues. How is a religion made? How does it function in people? So I decided it was necessary to do an *underview*, looking at religion from the ground up.

I came to a startling revelation. Religions are really human enterprises. But they are often dealt with, especially by the religious themselves, like objects instead of a human enterprise. The pretense is that they can be compared directly on key doctrinal points as though no people were involved.

But the truth is, where there are no people, there is no religion. Without people, there may be historical records, books, symbols, and artifacts, as in ancient Assyria, but the religion is dead. The more you see that religion exists only in the lives of people, the better you see it. A religion consists not so much in the outer things—the vestments, ceremony, in what is called God or the gods—but in how the most exemplary members of a religion live. So my effort at an overview evolved into looking at religions as essentially made of lives. The religious Beiruts of the world come about because opposing sides each conceive of themselves as absolutely correct; thereby they have a right to overlook the humanity of the other side and indeed may overlook even their own humanity in their dark struggle.

I view religious conflicts with a bitter sadness, as though our loftiest enterprise somehow was dropped and allowed to trail in the dirt. But cheer up. Seeing religion as really a human enterprise prevents much of this.

Culture, the Home of Religion

Our world is now so mixed up, so confused with instant communication, that we are in danger of losing the sense of the wonder of human culture. Go back just a century or so. Let us look in on a group of people, a tribe that has been a living entity for an unknown number of generations. They can number from ten or a hundred. As the group gets too big, it splits because such a large group too easily exhausts the foraging possibilities. The people in the group live together all their lives, are intimately interdependent, and evolve a culture. A culture is a marvelously complex way of dealing with everything: interpersonal relations, families, sexual roles, and how to live, build homes, and feed the members of the group. A culture is an adaptation of a group to its environment and to each other. The adaptation evolves and adapts to changing conditions. Reflect on the differences between the indigenous Eskimo in the Arctic and the Indian in the Amazon. Clothes, tools—every aspect of their cultures differs because one lives on ice and the other in a jungle. If we were fully accepted into either culture, we could get some general ideas of the cultural mores in perhaps a couple of years. And, in a year or so, we could begin to use their language. But to assimilate the more subtle and complex aspects of so foreign a culture could easily take decades. Even at that, we would have the disadvantage of having lived in another world. We would not have come to the culture in as subtle a way as an infant raised in it.

Yet there is a key that helps us to understand, even though each culture is unique. We are all *more human than otherwise.* We each eat, defecate, have sex, and enjoy the esteem of others. We are linked by our common humanity.

I saw a miniature culture form in groups brought together for therapy. There would be an initial feeling-out of each other and a testing of the leadership. Within hours, the group members were shaping up their agreed-upon mores. I became known for setting up therapeutic communities. I would take a ward of ninety or so patients and set the initial parameters of a living community. The members would elect their officers and start taking control over their own lives. They would first decide small issues. By solving issue after issue, they gradually became powerful patient communities.

I recall one particular meeting. The ward had been unlocked;

members could come and go. But we had admitted two people who were actively suicidal. Do we as staff lock up the unit or could the patients come up with a way to handle the situation? The patients developed a buddy system for those who were suicidal.

The tendency to form a culture is a universal attribute of human groups. It goes on in our modern cities, but that situation is complex. There are subcultures of neighborhoods, race, socio-economic groups, and families. A city dweller learns to shift from one culture to another.

We can now define religion in cultural terms: a religion is the group's best-garnered answer to ultimate issues such as birth and death. It answers questions such as what happens after we die. It deals with all aspects of the environment seen as More-than-Self. The definition of this "More" varies with technology. In a technological group (such as our own), weather is up to the meteorologists, and crops are the province of agriculture. In a pretechnological society, More can include the weather and crops, with these things in the realm of spirits and gods. And the cultural group will have people (priests, shamans) assigned to interpret to its members how to deal with all the More-than-Self. In a real sense, indigenous cultures usually have far more religion than we do because the More includes so much for them, much of which we have split off and handed to various experts.

But even with all of our science, there is much left over. What happens when we die, and how shall we handle death? Religion is the collected and safeguarded sacred wisdom of a group. It is the higher aspect of a culture, where the culture attempts to deal with ultimates. It contains the culture's highest ideals and biggest explanations. If you picture the long, slow, complex evolution of a culture, whether in an early stage (without a written language) or otherwise, and see religion as its highest aspect, you might get a sense of how great a cultural shock was provided by missionaries or other outsiders who would root up "pagan" practices and substitute religious insights that evolved in a remote and alien context. Too bad missionaries weren't more like anthropologists, whose desire is to understand and appreciate and not to change. I would be loath to alter what is already an ancient operating system, especially when I was far from understanding it.

In part, I see difficulty just in our use of words and concepts. I once saw a television program with a sensitive portrayal of two brothers who lived among the Javanese people and who spoke the language. They had gone to much trouble to meet with an isolated tribe in central Borneo. Since the tribe was nomadic and the jungle very difficult to travel in, one native guide used dream-travel to locate the tribe. In my studies, I had learned that dream-travel is possible; it is a form of lucid dreaming where one uses the extrasensory perception in dreams to find something. Having found the tribe, the two brothers lived with them for some months. The tribal members described heaven in their view. Heaven was like a jungle paradise, a dream world one enters when one dies, where all animals are friendly. The shaman predicted one of the brothers would have a big dream of this heaven. And he did. He found himself in an endless and gorgeous jungle where all the animals knew him and were friendly. He described his sense that he was in the midst of One Life everywhere.

Regardless of what name is given to this place, I recognize it too. Other than the jungle, it looks much like the heaven I have known. Only mine has houses. I am not put off by this apparent difference. To a man who has always known jungle, why shouldn't heaven be a jungle? Isn't heaven the highest of what we have known? I would recognize the indigenous tribesman who can dream-travel and find things, who knows of the jungle heaven, as a spiritual man, one with whom I would enjoy spending time. Would I prefer to travel in the jungle with a noted Western theologian or this barefoot native? In the jungle, I prefer the indigenous theology. I could survive with it. It is the better theology in the jungle context.

We are too easily put off by apparent differences. Heaven as a jungle? Obviously, the native is limited in his understanding! But is not my heaven with houses a similar limitation? To overcome these doctrinal differences, we need to get a feeling for how the tribesman's ideas are used in a human context. He calls his God-above-all by some name I never heard of before. I need to see how comprehensive his God is and how he treats this More-than-Self. If his relationship to his God bears any resemblance to mine, then I suspect his God is the same as mine. I need to empathize with his intent, his experience, and his use of concepts to see how they fit with my own experience. Meaning is not in words themselves but in how people use them. The life of religion is the life of people. I need to empathize with their lives to sense what their religious expressions mean. Then the stranger and I meet in our common humanity. Insofar as I come to live through his religion as he does, then I begin to understand. This process I call interiorization. No doctrine is properly understood externally. It must be part of my life before I can see its real nature.

Say my barefoot, jungle-dwelling friend who dream-travels and speaks of a jungle heaven also addresses the spirits of trees and plants. At first, this practice just seems odd. I need to know exactly how and why he does it and then interiorize the same process. It is only when I get into the process and begin to experience what he does in response to the plant that I can finally judge it as a religious element. By then it has begun to make so much sense that I don't see anything wrong with it. Many gardeners who have already found that it helps to talk to plants would have even less difficulty understanding the process. I cannot stand wholly outside another's experience and understand his encounter with the spiritual. When I enter the experiential basis of his religion, however, I come into empathy with him as a person, as human, as more like myself than different. The issues of really understanding an alien culture and an alien religion are much the same.

But words, names, and differences in language trick us into thinking there are far greater differences than there are. Because we are all human, and in this sense more alike than different, we are linked in a common humanity. The more I know of my own humanity, the better I can understand yours. It is our sameness—

or our oneness, if you will, despite differences. But to look further into this human basis of religion, we need to look closer at what the human really is.

The Design of Persons

In dealing with the design of persons, we are dealing with mystery pure and simple. This mystery is deepened and compounded by the fact that it is ourselves, what we are, and the basis of our understanding. We use our understanding to study understanding, and we rightly suspect any deficiency in our tool will result in a deficiency in our understanding. In dealing with a culture, our understanding is influenced socially. Why were men's and women's roles so assigned in a culture? Partly it must have been built on physical potentials. Women bear children and need a protected and nurturing environment. Meanwhile, the man can be out and about. This situation must help decide the roles. But, as we look at group differences, we see some variation in men's and women's roles, so the culture must have some freedom of choice in addition to the physical potentials of the male and female. Cultures can be explained as socially developed answers. The religious aspect of a culture may be less social because a religion is built on some learned technology (e.g., healing with herbs) and some personal revelations given to the leaders. The names of the spirits of plants and the forces around them are probably derived from big events (revelations) that are given to individuals. In this aspect of religion, we are closer to the mysteries of the human than we are to social problem solving of cultures in general.

To understand persons and how they relate to religion, let us consider the concept of the human. Although the real nature of the human is decidedly mysterious, we all have some intuitive appreciation of what it means. If it is said that a man is "very human," I would take it as a compliment. It says that he does not act in a restrained, socially expected way, but rather acts more carefree, as he feels, feeling free to reveal himself. His humanness should make others feel more at ease. His humanness suggests a casual, creative approach to the world. Yet I see humanness as also mysterious. It is as though humanness is a core mystery that is forever being manifested in different ways. Because it is so rich and variable, we can sense it, intuit it, even though we do not expect it to remain the same. We are human, and we sense a similar humanness in others. Appreciation of basic humanness allows us to look beyond social differences, age, sex, physical differences, and other incidental differences to the way we are essentially the same, even though this sameness is itself somewhat mysterious. In the concept of the human, I have an intuitive idea that sees a core likeness across infinite personal differences.

How does this relate to religion? Religions are human enterprises, our central theme and the title of this chapter. It is when we forget the human aspect and look at religions as odd objects that we come to the most serious misunderstandings. We become like the Inquisition, able to subject another to torture for the grave heresy of not saying things in the way we expect to hear them. Doctrinal arguments are like verbal traps. I have known followers of a religion whose understanding of doctrine becomes so razor sharp it turns out they are the only person on earth to really, really understand the truth. These people often become involved in paranoid plots, for they have figured out why everyone is so contrary to them. They become lonely churches of one.

Insofar as we enter into another's religious experience and feel it as a human process, an effort of a person to relate to and consult with the More-than-Self (whatever it is called), the more it makes simple human sense. Religions are very much an interior process. We must get into its human interior, to feel it as a simple human effort. Then the details of the artifacts used, the words—all the outer accoutrements of religion—fall into secondary importance. As it becomes human, like us, then it becomes understandable and even, in some respects, familiar. I would like to emphasize the word *interiorization*. It is the process of getting into all the interior ramifications of something. One must get into the interior of a culture to experience it as a comprehensive answer of a people as to how to live in a setting. One must interiorize a religion to get even a glimpse of its realities. Like getting into a culture, getting into a religion takes some time of careful empathy. In a few instances, one can interiorize a religion in moments. This can occur when one's own interior and that of the religion are seen to be the same. The more alien a religion is to one's very nature, the more difficult it is to interiorize. And it may be impossible. Suppose we have a withdrawn, monkish sort of person. Visualize him or her going to an inner-city black church, filled with singing, clapping, and vigorous self-expression. This person would look for the nearest exit. It would be a long and difficult road for him or her to interiorize such a religion. So our own nature conditions what is even possible to interiorize.

By addressing the human, we have provided the key by which we can find our way across differences, but now I would like to address differences as a central issue. My model of a person will end up with uniqueness set inside the generally human. In a paradoxical way, it is as though all our differences are an endless illustration of what it potentially means to be human. Just imagine we are sitting at the side of a very busy street with many people going by. We see a revelation from God passing before our eyes. Each face and each figure of each person passing by are different. If we could look closer, every voice, every movement are different. Every fingerprint is different. Magnified even further, every cell and each person's DNA are different. Whatever designed all this detail certainly enjoys endless differences. It reminds me of theme and variations in music. The theme is human, but each person is a different variation on the theme. The more people we see, the broader our intuition of what the underlying human theme is.

We need some way to capture the uniqueness of a person. In a real sense, Western science cannot do this. Science groups, classifies, and seeks norms. Everyone's uniqueness is then almost viewed as a fault, a departure from a norm. In the course of my explorations, I have found several ways of approaching uniqueness. The first and most obvious is simply to describe the person's life as a unique self. This is done in novels and stories. In clinical psychology, it is done in a case history. The philosophical idea of the nature of a person appealed to me even as a boy. In my attempt to understand a person, I would attempt to describe his or her nature. My own nature is always to seek to understand. Once a person's nature is understood, one is in a better position to predict their choices and how they would tend to experience life.

Within existential psychology, I was impressed by phenomenology; this is a radical attempt to describe the uniqueness of a person's world. Phenomenology has no assumptions about what is good or bad, normal or not; rather, it is about unique worlds. It was in a phenomenological description of a patient's world that I had a real sense I was beginning finally to see mental illness. For instance, I have a friend who was a long-term patient in a mental hospital. Somehow we hit it off, so I view him as a friend rather than as a patient. But his world was pervaded by sickness. We'd walk in the garden, and I would point out a particularly healthy-looking flower and say, "Surely this doesn't look sick." But, yes, it did to him. To him everything was pervaded by a kind of cancerous distortion. Our relationship consisted of his forever trying to help me see this pervasive disease, while I tried to help him see health. Neither of us succeeded. We were in different worlds.

Phenomenology discovers the total uniqueness of an individual's world. It is as though we are each in a personal world. Though our worlds meet and interact, they remain different.

There is an allied idea that comes from Swedenborg: each person is seen as having a unique love of life, which is a given, central ruling tendency that subtly conditions all experience:

> *Our love is our life. Whatever our love is like, that is what our life is like—in fact, that is what our whole self is like.*
> *Bur out primary or controlling love is what makes us the person we are. This love has many subordinate loves that*

come from it. These loves appear in different ways outwardly, but all of them fit in with the primary love and make one realm with it. The primary love is like their ruler and head. It guides them and uses them as intermediate goals in aiming for and working toward its own goal, which is the primary, underlying one. It does this in both direct and indirect ways. Our primary love is whatever we love more than anything else.

Whatever we love more than anything else is constantly present in our thinking and our motivation. It is the central nature of our life. Here are a couple of examples:

If we love wealth more than anything else, whether it is money or possessions we want, we are always turning over in our minds how we can obtain it for ourselves. We feel very happy when we gain wealth, and very sad when we lose it, because our heart is in it.

If we love ourselves more than anything else, we keep ourselves in mind in every little detail. We think about ourselves, talk about ourselves, and do things for our own benefit, because our life is a selfish one.[2]

Swedenborg's love of life is similar to seeing a person's nature. I prefer his definition because it implies a great deal about the operation of this central tendency. It is more like feeling one's love than it is like thinking. It conditions what one perceives, what one gravitates toward. Swedenborg describes the love of the life of each person as unique and as lasting through all the worlds. We cannot know it directly since it amounts to the divine core of the person, but certainly we can sense our own general drift and that of others. I have a friend who is a Roman Catholic mystic. Over decades, I have sensed her life circling around a mystical interest. She has evolved a form of prayer she calls "carrying a wisdom melody." It

---

2. Emanuel Swedenborg, *The Heavenly City: A Spiritual Guidebook*, trans. Lee Woofenden (West Chester, Penna.: Swedenborg Foundation, 1993), paragraphs 54–55.

consists of silently repeating a phrase such as "the power of love" and looking toward discoveries in the mystery of love. It is not mysticism in general, but it is rather her own unique way of mysticism within a general Roman Catholic framework. Should she lose this central striving, I would be very concerned about her health because it is her essence. Though I cannot know her love of life directly, I must certainly be close to seeing its nature and its tendencies. I do not know it all, nor does she, for it seems to evolve along its own lines.

It helps very much to see the uniqueness of another person, whether this is called their nature, the love of their life, or the design of their personal world. From this standpoint, the other person (and one's self) makes considerable sense. One is no longer surprised that the other person prefers to do this rather than that, that they occupy themselves in thus-and-so, that they notice thus-and-so aspects of the world and overlook other aspects. They seem a coherent and reasonable whole. I understand myself in this way also.

But it may seem paradoxical that I now have elaborated two almost opposite tendencies in humans. In the first, we are all more human than otherwise, and this is the basis on which I can empathize with others. The opposite is that each has a different nature or love of life, from which each forms a personal world. Swedenborg put these together in a single image—the Grand Man.

The Grand Man is an image of heaven in the form of a single person. Heaven is made of societies that function together like organs in its body. Our innate, God-given (since we don't design them) natural tendencies place us somewhere in the Grand Man. In doing what we innately most love to do, we contribute our part to the Grand Man. The Grand Man is the One Life, the Divine Human. This is a representation of the nature of heaven. In heaven each does what he or she most dearly and innately loves to do, thereby contributing to the One Life. I could bring this image down to the earthly level, and it still remains true. Societies on earth are made up of people in an immense variety of roles. The mother takes care of her children, or there will not be a future. This one cleans, that one repairs, and the other does heaven knows what; but all contribute. Is anyone really more important than another? I doubt it. The "lowly" garbage collector needs only to go on strike to impress us with his or her importance.

What has individual uniqueness to do with religion? Though we are all more human than otherwise, we are also, mysteriously, unique. Visualize people passing by on a busy street. View everyone as different and use this as a revelation as to the nature of More-than-Self that seems to like endless differences. The endless variety of religions reflects both Oneness (called at the human level, humanness) and variety. I will speak later in this chapter of the oneness of religion. It is easier to understand the variety of religions. In a small group of indigenous people, we saw uniformity of religion, although, even in a group of twenty people or so who had always lived together, we would still find on close examination religious differences. There would be differences in belief and differences in depth of interiorization. As we move across cultures, we begin to see surprising differences. Now in a technologically advanced world, where we are flooded with instant communication, the variety of religions becomes incredible. This endless variety occurs, even if we examine in depth the people of one given religion. As I said before, the endless differences are a kind of revelation of the nature of things.

In case you are not yet sufficiently impressed with differences, then let me tell you about religions that are not even considered to be religions. I have a friend who likes to tease me about my religious interest. He himself is an agnostic. Agnosticism seems reasonable and practical to me. If God would show up and sufficiently impress my friend, my friend would acknowledge him. But not having met the gentleman (if God is a male), my friend does not believe. He is a retired forester who worked all his life with trees. Now, the high point of his life is backpacking into the country. There he spends hours getting just the right light to photograph flowers. I enjoy his slides because they show his love for flowers. One day when he was kidding me about my religious interests, I asked when he planned the next trip to his church of the Yosemite high country. He was taken aback just for a moment, but he recognized my point. His church is up in the mountains. It has a central symbol—a flower. His God is called Nature. He shows what is to me the most fundamental aspect of religious devotion—respect and awe toward what is More-than-Self. It looks remarkably like a religious practice. I sense the same thing in a great many other human endeavors. I have known mothers for whom the raising of children was a sacred duty. I find an immense kinship with artists pursuing beauty and the mysteries of creativity. I have known the same sense of awe in scientists. In short, I believe that if we look at religion as a human process, we have many more religions than we suspect.

What then are the central marks of what I would call a religion as a human process?

(1) It is a way for the individual to relate to what he or she experiences as the More-than-Self.

(2) This personal way contains mystery, awe, pleasure, and the sense of growth or development, however slow, toward the More.

I see explanation (theology, doctrine, etc.) as secondary, and it may be tacit and implied rather than explicit; that is, I do not see the religious explanation as a central mark. Rather in the center is some way of relating to what the individual perceives of the More-than-Self. It is a personal approach to a larger reality. The perceived More-than-Self to the artist may be beauty, or to a birder, birds. In the center, I see individuals attempting to relate to the More-than-Self that strikes them. Here the individual love of life plays a role. Depending upon our natures, we perceive different aspects of the More-than-Self. My pious backpacking friend sees it most clearly in natural beauty. I know a woman whose perception of the More-than-Self is not apparent until it comes to a hurt animal. Then she is mobilized to the greatest extent to help the animal.

Let me pinpoint what is involved in dealing with the opposite.

I call religion any human way of respectfully dealing with the perceived More-than-Self. Its opposite is well described by Swedenborg as hell. Those who end up in hell have done it to themselves, basically by not having any More-than-Self. They are the center of their universe. Only they matter. Everything and everyone else are in a lesser position. There simply is no More-than-Self to relate to. As a result, their world tends to spiral inward on itself. By contrast, in heaven the world opens out to something More; the human experience opens, expands. The implication in hell is that things can close down and constrict. And, as a result, the person in hell is in conflict with all the More. On earth, it is like the criminal who sets him- or herself too high and comes into conflict with the rights of others. The implication of the opening out, evolving expansion of heaven is that More can be found.

I am quite aware that some will say that one must have a God as the More-than-Self, or religion does not exist. These same people often have difficulty if someone does not have a God of the same name as theirs (i.e., Christ, Brahman, Allah, Buddha). They also have difficulty with multiple gods. There has to be only one, or it does not count. As a human experience, multiple gods usually mean simply that the various aspects of the More have been differentiated. Most people with multiple gods also have a supreme One. Multiple gods are very like praying to the Virgin Mary regarding female matters and to Saint George regarding safety in battle. Religion seems to have an unfortunate tendency to find fault with differences. The aspect that has caused more deaths than any other is around the issue of the "one true religion," which I will now examine.

The One True Religion

As a matter of fact, I do believe there is one true religion, but it is a spiritual reality. It cannot be totally identified with any one religion on earth. As a spiritual or an interior reality, it is whatever brings a person into relationship with the More-than-Self. If you think for a moment, isn't it reasonable that some individuals in every religion have probably found their way to God? We are, of course, dealing with mysteries beyond our full understanding. But intuitively I suspect at least some people of every religion have found their way to the More-than-Self. Conversely, no matter how wondrous our own particular religion is, we are likely to know scoundrels in it whose ultimate destiny we would not care to share. That is, it seems likely that no religion functions perfectly to provide the highest ultimate destiny to all, regardless of conduct or lack of effort. This is a central point in Swedenborg. Faith alone does not save. Rather our destiny is based upon the total quality of life and what we have done.

I believe we can put an even finer point on this argument. Many religions say religious practice must be done exactly their way. Many imply that, if you do not find their religion and do things exactly their way, you are condemned to hell. This view seems grossly unreasonable because a great many persons have not even had contact with their particular religion. I suspect that a person's destiny is related more to the quality of the effort than it is to discovering precisely the right way. If you doubt this idea, pretend to be God and decide how you would deal with a mentally handicapped person who arrives at heaven's gates. Are you still a stickler for details? And, in a larger sense, are we not all mentally challenged?

If we look at it in a human sense, I believe the concept of one true religion means several things. The person enunciating that there is only one true religion is really saying his or her religion works completely for him or her. When authorities in a religion say the same thing, it often means that they find their religion works for them and that they believe it can work for anyone. But this view is suspect. It overlooks the great range of human differences. Can it work for the mentally challenged, the drug-using-rock-and-roll-teenager, the person raised in a different culture? Very often, we can see a religion functioning best for an ethnic group or better for one age group. There are a number of religions that attract the better educated. I know of no example where a religion works equally well for all people. Even within a religious culture, we see great differences in how well it takes. My Roman Catholic mystical friend can give an able dissertation on the difficulties of being a mystic in her church.

Down through history, we have seen many examples of religion being imposed on others "because it is good for them." This certainly happened both in the Christian and in the Muslim traditions. Take any religion and reflect for a moment on what it would be like if it became the only one permitted in the whole world. Can you conceive of such a thing as even possible? No matter how well it were spread, there would be enclaves here and there in rebellion. In Central America, it would quietly become mixed with ancient indigenous beliefs. There would be struggles in the church hierarchy, one group calling others heretics. To my mind, the universal realization of one religion would be a cultural disaster of incredible proportions.

But, in a human sense, there is one true religion. It is all that immense variety of things that brings one into a relationship with the More. Here it functions this way, there that way. Isn't it a delight and a wonder how many ways there are, almost a way for each person, the revelation foretold by the endless differences in faces? I find great delight when I find others have creatively found a way I had not anticipated. I believe in the Eastern Orthodox (and in many other religious) ideas of deification—that we should each strive to become God. I do not see the variety of religions as a fault, as though some gross misunderstanding has intruded. Rather I see it as a partial illustration of an even deeper truth. There are endless ways to relate to the More. Depending upon our own life experience and our God-given, innate tendencies, we each find our way. It is a Hindu concept that we are all climbing the same mountain, but we find different paths to the top. Some paths are a little longer than others, some harder to climb; but in the end none of this matters. We are, after all, dealing with eternity, and this little time here is not much. We certainly have a right to say what suits us individually. It is when we overlook the vast array of differences and want to impose our way on others that we make a serious mistake. Moreover, it cannot be done. It is the shortest way to war.

Instead, I opt for the rich texture of variability and differences we see in existence. It is not so variable that we cannot see patterns. Among these patterns are ourselves. Looking across ourselves, we see a basic similarity. And beyond that, there is an interdependence and unity of all life. Not far beyond that is the One that conceived this most creative and impressive design.

Summary

We began with religion as the carefully garnered wisdom of a culture. Religion, like a culture, is a slowly evolved wisdom regarding the ultimates. Across cultures, we, at first sight, see differences in religions; but if we look at their hearts as functional human processes, we begin to sense their intrinsic similarity. Despite the impediment of all my Western learning, I would hope I could live with a Borneo tribe, learn dream-walking, and experience the illumination of a jungle heaven. Apparently opposite to the fact that we are all more human than otherwise are our endless differences. Like the great variety of human faces, we each seem designed from beyond ourselves with a central love of life. This love conditions our desires, our perceptions, and ultimately the design of our personal world. Fortunate indeed are the people who find and live out their love. Religions in their variety serve our immense differences. Yet each, in its way, points beyond itself to the More. I had to use a broad term such as the More to get beyond the various names of God and even beyond what was called religion.

As a human experience, the essence of "religion" is to find a way to open ourselves respectfully to the More-than-Self, a path that meets the individual's unique love of life. But because I am human, I can empathize with, understand, and respect others' ways. For somehow there really is but One Life, and we are interacting expressions of it. All expressions of the One Life are welcome. We are composed of the More, embedded in the More, and led to the More. I agree with the many religions that say all will be saved—humans, animals, plants, rocks, all. For this is another way of saying that ultimately it is All One. My purpose here has been to try to bring more tolerance of parts of the More toward other parts by showing religion as basically a human process. Insofar as we enjoy our own humanity, we should enjoy others also. How well our differences enrich existence. We may as well learn to accept differences, for it is in the very nature of things. It is a wonderful paradox that, by enjoying the rich fabric of differences, we begin to see the Oneness of it all.[3]

---

3. For an excellent presentation of this outlook on religion, see William Paden, *Religious Worlds* (Boston: Beacon Press, 1984) and *Interpreting the Sacred* (Boston: Beacon Press, 1992).

Chapter Five

The Mystic's View of Salvation

I AM QUITE CONVINCED MYS-
tics benefit from the company of other mystics. After all, quilters get together, as do gun collectors, automobile aficionados, etc. It is edifying to meet someone else with your same interest and share your joys, experiences, and ideas. For mystics, it is as though we have all visited the same vast and varied country—perhaps Mystis, as I mentioned earlier. We can share different aspects of that country and, by our sharing, come to new insights about the spiritual world.

The only trouble with mystics getting together is that there are so few of us, too few to make up an association. Now, as I have said previously, I believe that the actual number of people who have had some sort of mystical experience is vast, clearly in the millions. But there is quite a difference between those who had some experience of God and those who have lived in this experience for some time and have published on it. The process of publishing implies (1) sufficient breadth of experience to have more than a moment or two to report and (2) the selection of edifying experiences. Ancient published accounts that are still available imply considerable selection by people over time.

Evelyn Underhill did a fine, complete reporting on all the published mystics in the Western world in the last 2000 years.[1] She lists eighty-seven. If we add Jesus and several Sufi mystics, such as Jalāl AD-Dīn AR-Rūmī whom Underhill did not include, this list grows to perhaps ninety-three. This means that there is a published mystic every 21.5 years on average. Actually, the number of literary mystics bunch up in the Middle Ages when many spiritually oriented people lived a monastic life. Unfortunately, contemporary published mystics in the western world are rare. We can't easily gather together and have a convention. The best we can do is to read the work of past mystics. So, I have gradually accumulated and have long enjoyed my library of published mystics, East and West.

It was while comparing mystics that I gradually formulated the central question of this chapter—"Who is saved?" When I read the great Christian mystic Emanuel Swedenborg, I find a most liberal answer: all are saved who live by the good they know. To bring out Swedenborg's intent, I must stress the phrase "live by." Clearly, in the context of his thirty volumes of theological writings, Swedenborg means that we are saved according to how we *really* live. Being good in the last ten minutes of life is helpful but not necessarily enough. The "good they know" implies a kind of universal tolerance. He is clearly not saying one must be Christian. A pagan, acting in the good of his or her culture, will be saved.

Let me clarify what the term "to be saved" means. In evangelical Christianity, it has taken on the meaning of a person's having experienced a very emotional state in which he or she has taken Christ as personal savior. But, like mystics East and West, I see a

---

1. Evelyn Underhill, *Mysticism* (New York: Dutton, 1961). The listing appears in the bibliography.

deeper meaning in salvation. *Being saved or salvation is not a simple, all at once, it-is-done process.* Rather salvation begins when we sense there is an Ultimate, More-than-Self in which our lives are embedded. You are on the eternal Way when you see this and begin relating to this More. Normally, Westerners would simply say a person relates to God or Christ. I used the above formulation of relating to the Morje-than-Self to open up the idea to include Hindu and Buddhist conceptions of the Ultimate. The common idea that salvation is easy, immediate, and lifelong is a childlike simplification. Instead we come to relate to the More-than-Self in this life and through all the lives to come. In an eternal perspective, I can then see that, whatever my conception of salvation is now, it is likely to change and evolve through this life and the next. So, it includes the idea of having come into relationship with a mystery whose scope, meaning, and future direction I don't really understand. There is a kind of presumption in any declaration of "I am saved" (which often means that others are not) and, worse yet, in any idea that I fully understand what this means now and ever into the future.

I have often remarked that salvation lies in the direct experience of God, i.e., in becoming a mystic. But even this statement needs some elaboration. I see anyone who has come into even a momentary experience of God as having started on the process. The experience is so uplifting and enlightening that there is a natural curiosity as to how to return to it. Hence, the person has begun on his or her way to God. I am thinking of a vast time span. So, a person might have a momentary experience in this life, forget, and neglect it for the rest of his or her life, but in the process of dying, come back to the experience of God.

The Tibetan Buddhists, as master explorers in this area, have been aware for centuries of what we have just discovered in the West, the near-death experience. For most people, the near-death experience is almost an automatic return to enlightenment and the experience of God. Because this is true, the Tibetan Book of the Dead was written as a guide to the dying.[2] It is actually read to a person before, during, and after dying, in an effort to make the best possible use of the process of dying. In no respect am I critical of the Tibetan Buddhist tradition. The use of the Book of the Dead is for those who have been raised in a Buddhist tradition. It is implied that they will understand *bardo*s (which are different inner states, i.e., the dream *bardo* is the state of being in a dream) and all the traditional Buddhist elements in the book.

It was when I contrasted Swedenborg's assertion that all will be saved who act on the good they know to the Tibetan almost meticulous care around the time of death that I was struck by the contrast. The Western Christian way to let death happen is in sharp contrast to the Tibetan Book of the Dead's care to get the maximum benefit from the process of dying. In addition, I found Bokar Rinpoche's more inner and spiritual description of the dying process quite helpful.[3] What I was struck by is the cultural difference of Swedenborg's liberal approach to the Tibetan's almost fussy concern over all the complexity of stages. I realize that, in part, these are cultural differences in approach, not necessarily real spiritual differences. For Swedenborg, when we die, we come into the hands of the living God, in whose hands we have been all along. In contrast, the Tibetans have a penchant for a vast and detailed examination of inner states and particularly spiritual states.[4]

If I call on my experience as a mystic, I can resolve the apparent difference between Swedenborg's liberality and the Tibetan's meticulous work with the experience of dying. Indeed, I believe both work and are appropriate.

---

2. Sogyal Rinpoche, *The Tibetan Book of Living and Dying* (San Francisco: Harper Collins, 1992).

3. Bokar Rinpoche, *Death and the Art of Dying* (San Francisco: Clear Point Press, 1993). *Rinpoche* is a Tibetan Buddhist religious title meaning "precious one."

4. I regard the Communist Chinese's systematic destruction of the people, religion, culture, and country of Tibet as one of the great losses of this century. Tibet is the sanctuary of some of the most advanced mystical understanding in existence. The compassionate work of the Dalai Lama and his people is helping to lessen this cultural loss. The Communist Chinese have no idea what they are really doing.

We have here a cultural difference. The Christians simply haven't looked at the process of dying, and so they have less to say about it. Buddhists, on the other hand, have explored the process of death for centuries, so they have devised a way for the person to be guided through it and to make the best use of the experience. Swedenborg's is less detailed but would work for a Christian. At the moment of dying, Christians give themselves over to Christ, an experience they should have already been through countless times in church services and in prayer. The Tibetan way is for those raised in that culture.

Thus, we need not be put off at all by cultural differences but rather try to see into their spirit and to learn from them. But all this is really just the backdrop for a more serious question about who is saved. In effect, we have accepted various religious ways to approach the eternity we enter upon by dying. But suppose the person dies and shows not a trace of religion. What then? Some would readily say that such a person would be condemned to hell. Not necessarily. Let me take the case of the friend of mine whom I mentioned earlier and extrapolate to his eternity. I take him as a model example. Actually, I use him because I will tell him he is in this book, and that is the only way I could get him to ever look at anything spiritual!

My Friend the Outdoorsman

Bud is a thin, wiry man of the outdoors. He has been my neighbor and friend for years. We drive two hours to concerts frequently. During these long drives, we have an ample chance to chatter and share views. I am not usually much of a talker, but I can be loquacious when expounding on spiritual matters. Bud talks less and patiently listens.

Bud is a dyed-in-the-wool agnostic. That is, he is not opposed to God; but having never experienced God, he has trouble believing in a deity. Bud is a well-trained scientist, having enjoyed a career in forestry. He and I read the same science magazine, and on our trips to concerts, we have been all over the known universe in our discussions. We enjoy talking about black holes and what the unknown dark matter may be. We both delight in the range of scientific findings.

We also seem to fall into a natural relationship of male banter. He is a runner. Sometimes he visits my home full of bouncy vigor after having warmed up over a fourteen-mile run. Meanwhile, I am partly paralyzed and have trouble just walking. This has led to all sorts of jokes. Bud has just turned seventy; for him, the real meaning of this event is that he is now the youngest in his age-class in races. He looks forward to beating other seventy-year-olds! Since he is immensely ambitious in running, I have often goaded him to trying the hundred-mile run over the Sierra Nevada Mountains, offering to carry his drink bottle on my motorcycle.

Bud knows quite well that I am a mystic and a writer. On our concert trips, he has allowed me hours to roam over the entire field. To him religion is like someone reporting on strange life in an alien universe; it simply makes no real or personal sense to him. Bud is really an outdoorsman. He backpacks in remote parts of national parks. In retirement, he now lovingly takes pictures of flowers. He knows the names of each and knows details of their lives; he has been known to amaze flower clubs with his slide presentations. In our natural kind of competitive male banter, we try to get each other in an argument. I got him one day on the matter of religion.

When I expound on religion, he is quite tolerant, almost like an anthropologist trying to understand some unusual indigenous practice. We had arrived back home after a concert and were about to depart to our respective homes. He had just expressed again the sentiment that religion makes no sense to him. He was about to go on another backpacking trip to his beloved mountains. I turned and said, "That is the cathedral where you worship. Enjoy the services." I got him! That really took him aback. To amplify this idea, on subsequent trips, I analyzed the parallels between his trips and his pictures of flowers and ordinary worship. Bud's God is called Nature, as I mentioned previously. He respects it greatly and has always enjoyed all his contacts with it. His affection led him into the occupation of forestry in the first place.

So now I can come down to my basic question. My friend Bud represents millions of people. His friends will all agree he is a good, considerate, ethical person. After years of contact, I can't think of any real sins in him. Yet he is about as irreligious as anyone can get. Religion to him seems to be an alien enterprise. Although he is tolerant of others' beliefs, religion simply makes no sense to him.

So, what about Bud and eternity? In the first place, he qualifies for salvation under Swedenborg's dictum: he acts by the good he knows. The real good he knows is Nature. As a forester, he questioned whether trees could be harvested, and he was in favor of sustainable yields and the preservation of forest as much as possible. The real hang-up for most people on the question of his salvation is that Bud doesn't believe in God; he can't believe in what he hasn't seen. He has seen nature and respects its complexity and the interdependence of all life forms. Those who make a belief in God central are, to my mind, equally hung up on a concept that even they must admit is full of mystery. It makes them doubt Buddhists who have no "God" but instead point to a state, *nirvana,* which in plain Western terms is a state full of God.

Suppose for a moment we substitute for the Western God a term that has occasionally been used, the *Real.* Let us define the Real as what exists ultimately and eternally. The Real is substantial in the philosophical sense, existing in itself, not dependent on anything else. Now suppose a man believing in the Real takes tangible things as signs of this Real. Or, better yet, he doesn't accept any object; instead he most honors the real that is so much a part of his own nature that he would be bereft not to find, honor, and relate to this Real. My outdoor friend has found this Real that resonates inwardly with him, so Bud is not just honoring some external golden calf but the outward Real for which he has the greatest depth of feeling. An agnostic woman acquaintance of mine honors beautiful design. She could hardly do otherwise; it is a part of her nature. The real spiritual is always both inward and outward, and the two are in a kind of resonating process whereby the inner gives meaning to the outer and the outer reminds and enlivens the inner.

So what about Bud's eternal? All mystics report that it is the aim of God to lead all back into the fullness of God. If you were God, how would you accomplish this in Bud's case? The process is already underway. Bud worships a God called Nature. How to catch Bud's eye when he dies? It is easy. Usher him into a natural landscape of great beauty. Let him look, smell, and lovingly examine all the new flowers he has not seen before. Through this he can be led into all the Ultimates. I was correct when I said he is already going to church. His cathedral is immense; it has the sky itself for a ceiling.

Who is saved? All those who act on the good they know. This definition not only cuts across religions, but it also cuts across what some call religious and not religious. I don't need to convert Bud. He is already on a perfectly respectable Way, appropriate to him, likewise most other agnostics. Of course, I will keep kidding Bud when he is off to his cathedral of the mountains. Come to think of it, I should worship there more often myself.

The Religion That Is Not Called Religion

I used the case of Bud to broaden the discussion as to who is saved. Now I intend to broaden further into the area of life that functions like religion and yet bears none of the signs, symbols, or terms of religion. A theme that runs through almost all religions is to love one another, or do unto others as you would have them do unto you. Let us simplify this as the dictum to love one another and all creation. I broaden this to include creation because some people have been so hurt by humans that they have difficulty trusting others, but they can still love some aspect of creation, be it plant, animal, landscapes, or whatever. In a real sense, the underlying spirit is similar: to love, honor, care for, or respect what is more than yourself. We have so much More-than-Self about us that the choices are almost endless. For instance, I recall an agnostic astronomy professor I once had, and in particular, a moment in his introductory course. He had described in a series all the known motions in the universe. Why did a moment in a lecture a half century ago stand out to me? It was the way he expressed himself. I could see he loved and honored the cosmos. For him, the recitation of planetary motions wasn't just facts. He was *showing* his love. Astronomy is his key to the larger universe. Upon dying, he might be shown the wonder of the cosmos as his way into the spiritual.

My mother (bless her) had a very hard life. Her own mother had an explosive temper. When my mother was stabbed with scissors by her mother, she fled her home at the age of sixteen. Although she had been taught in Catholic schools, she was an angry agnostic who frequently said that, if God existed, he must be unspeakably cruel. Yet, under poverty and difficult circumstances, my mother clearly gave her life to her children. We became the More-than-Self to which she was devoted. Indeed, all of the agnostics I have cited were ethical persons, having no more than the usual flaws and sins. I would contend that, even in the ordinary canons of most of the world's religions, they would be saved, that their devotion to something larger than themselves—whether it be nature, art, astronomy, or their own children—would be their way into the spiritual. They would enter upon the Love of All from their more limited love.

These people, whom I believe are saved, contrast sharply with those whom Swedenborg contends are destined for hell.[5] However subtle or disguised those destined for hell are, inwardly they are

---

5. See the sections on spirits in hell, chapters 56 to 63, in Swedenborg's *Heaven and Hell,* trans. George F. Dole (West Chester, Penna.: Swedenborg Foundation, 1976).

focused on themselves over others. They are for self only. This type of person includes the politician who makes impressive speeches as to how he or she is going to help the country, but whose inner aim is getting power, not in helping the country. Swedenborg described with disappointment eminent bishops and the like that he met in hell. The spiritual world is, in effect, the realm of the real truth. In terms of our outer observation, the difference between good and evil can be subtle, especially where there is an effort to deceive. The spiritual can quite naturally sort out these differences and reveal true motivations and character.

But I can well understand some religions' objecting to my saving the non-religious whose lives, though commendable, don't bother with religion. There is a difference between the scope of Bud's life—or even that of the astronomy professor—and my mother's and those who enjoy religion. Those who participate in a religion may live a life of wider scope than agnostics who live a life of loving something more than themselves. We have to look at religious experience spiritually to see what I am referring to. Many go to church to be with friends, and the effect is not greatly different from being in any voluntary association. However, for those who really enter upon and experience a religion, as a truly spiritual enterprise, I do see an advantage in the scope of their existence.

It is one thing to be an ethical person devoted to a love of something more than oneself and another to be a functioning member of religion. A living religion provides a wider base of experience. The Hindu, for instance, is functioning in an ancient tradition that includes millions of people. The religious also have a way to get behind the screen of existence to deal with the Ultimate because religious doctrine provides an explanation of the total nature and purpose of existence. Thus, I truly believe that the religious may enjoy a wider scope of existence.

Let us arrange all the people we have dealt with here in a rough continuum. We shall see that, along this continuum, we are really dealing with shifts in both the scope and quality of existence. At one end of the continuum, we have those in hell. Their inner orientation is for themselves uppermost. If we take Swedenborg's *Heaven and Hell* as our standard, we should not think of them as being punished by God since Swedenborg makes clear that those in hell have gone to what they were accustomed to, to what they expected and desired. Compared to spirits in heaven, their existence is mean, limited, and full of interpersonal stresses, but this is a direct consequence of their choices. Hellish spirits live in what they have created and are familiar with.

The next level up are the agnostics who live an ethical life, devoted to something more than themselves; people such as Bud who worships in the cathedral of Nature. They are not religious because religion makes no immediate sense. They don't believe in a God they have not seen. The scope and quality of these people's existence widen out because they enjoy something more than themselves. I contend that these people in their ethical lives, and in enjoying something more than themselves, are on the way into the spiritual. They lack the gifts of religion, but they are at the entrance to the spiritual. And who knows—some have perhaps a truer religion than many of the so-called religious, for example, the agnostic of my acquaintance who enjoys beauty so much that she is almost always in her "church."

Next in our continuum are the religious for whom religion really has an internal function. Without this function, they simply resemble the ethical agnostics. An advantage I see here is this religious group enjoys (1) an ancient tradition, (2) an explanation of life and death, (3) and a means to contact and relate to the Ultimate. At least in these respects, their existence widens out in meaning and harmony.

Lastly, we have the small group of mystics who have the direct experience of God. Their personal existence has started to widen out to its Ultimates. This group may overlap with the truly religious described above. Mystics share the same pleasures of being in a tradition, having an explanation of the most important questions, and having a way to deal with Ultimates. They often lose all fear of death. The stresses of having a personal identity begin to fade for this group.

Back to our main question: who is saved? As we have seen, we can say all are saved who have come into the love of something more than themselves. The saving certainly begins in this life. Coming to love something more than ourselves, we have already entered on a wider existence in this world. Our lives are bigger, deeper, more meaningful, and more enjoyable than if we lived loving only the narrow confines of our own being. We are on our way, a journey that simply carries over into the next life. To me, this is the essence of a religious life, whether or not it has the name of God or religion on it.

From this larger perspective, I believe there are few who are not saved and that those few should have our sympathy and aid where we can help them. The Lord probably loves far beyond our little understanding and may find some good in all to work with. This would not surprise me. There is a doctrine in the Eastern Orthodox Church that asserts all will be saved, even plants, animals, and rocks, absolutely all. It is a lovely concept. I might personally hesitate on a few people but would gladly welcome all the rest of existence. This Eastern Orthodox belief is the Christian parallel to the Advaita Vedanta Hindu central doctrine that there is only Brahman. God is all there is, and this sweeps into its scope absolutely all of existence. What a beautiful concept. Ultimately all are saved. And those who enter upon the love of more than themselves are then beginning, in varying degrees, to enter upon this realization.

In a practical way, I see function as a critical issue in religion. Too many argue about abstract doctrine as though they manipulate simple objects outside themselves. It isn't like that at all. If we regard function, we are looking at a life wisdom that fully involves us. Salvation is a functional concept. I see a functional use in the concern for salvation, especially as it sets before us how we can actually further the scope, meaning, and joy in our lives. There is an inner similarity between agnostics who love something more than themselves and the religious enterprise itself.

As an inner and functional matter, salvation means to come to a way of relating to what is more than one's self, a way that can open out to Ultimates. But, if we are honest, we have to recognize that we don't fully know what we really are, yet alone the full mystery of the larger-than-ourselves that we try to get along with. The essence of this situation seems to lie in simply and humanly *trying*, rather than in a foolish doctrinal certainty, which is really belied by the mystery of every moment. And if the essence is in trying, let us admit to salvation all who try by any means they have.

I see two apparently contradictory ways in this. In our experience of human time, there is a valuable functional need for the idea of salvation or what one needs to do to participate in the All. But in eternity, it seems quite natural that all are simply aspects of the Eternal One, and in that sense all are saved in the One. Both are true. In time, there is struggle and development; but in the eternal, all rest in the One. And both can be simultaneously true. We can sense the eternal as the end already present, towards which struggling creatures move. The end is already real and present, or we would not have a sense that being saved is possible. There is an issue of the balance between these in each individual life. One person is nearer the pure struggle, while another is closer to realization.

This is what life is all about. In this life, we are in time and in a schoolhouse. Each student is trying to learn at his or her own pace and in his or her own way. Each has a concept of graduation, which is salvation. Each effortful attempt is inside the eternal potential of salvation—one inside the other. That is why we understand salvation from present intimations of it. This is the function of religion: to reveal ends and make them more real, to give intimations of the Ultimate.

As a human process, salvation begins when we realize we come from, and are embedded in, a More-than-Self, which is ever present and is here instructing us in the vicissitudes of life. By our trying and learning from the Ultimate, we enter upon a relationship to the All. We are saved moment by moment and eternally as we realize and attempt to live in harmony with the More-than-Self. To be saved is to come into harmony with all that is. In a temporal sense, salvation is a developmental process. But in eternity, it is already achieved. Eternity in the spiritual world is not endless time but rather a steady Presence. So there is the appearance of effort and growth (the lesser view) inside of what always is. This becomes clearer as we dwell on the eternal as already present. The eternal end manifests in the developing drama in time.

Chapter Six

Subtle Understanding: A Poem

*I've been through this
countless times,
for decades,
but it only recently
became clear.*

*Beneath rational understanding,
where we are conscious,
and full of words,
and things are relatively specific—
there is a whole different level
of understanding.
It is subtle.
It has less form,
no words,*

less specifics.
It is full of feeling,
of intuition,
of implied portents.
It is probably at this instinctive level
that animals operate
and plants blossom.
A mother uses it
as her primary guide,
in caring for her child.
Weather systems,
all natural phenomena,
operate on this level.
Indeed,
we alone
can be estranged
from this way of living.

For us,
this level requires compassion
with whatever we
wanted to understand.
At this compassionate level,
we merge with
all that is presented to us.
We and it are not separate.
It is full of love
and, arising out of that,
subtle understanding.
Understanding follows love.

Subtle understanding
is of a different nature
than rational analysis,
which must eliminate feeling,

to leave logic free.
Subtle understanding
enters with feeling
and very gradually
comes to understand.

I've lived
in subtle understanding
for decades now.
It is the basis
of the mystical,
the direct experience of God.
For God lives
in subtle understanding.

That is why,
when God showed me
the creation of the universe,
done so effortlessly,
I wondered where
was rational planning.
Subtle understanding
contains laws and order,
just as the body has bones.
God's subtle understanding
is enough to form
all the details,
all the interdependent interactions,
of the created universe.
God doesn't fuss
over the details.
Having in mind
the End of creation
is enough.

And why do I discover this
now?
That I and others
may come to respect
this level of function.

When we aren't stressed,
uptight,
and frantic—
But rather relaxed
and casual,
we too,
can move
with subtle understanding.
This level asks no questions,
because it answers all.
Patiently,
things become clear.
And what hurry
is there in eternity?
The way to knowing
all there is,
simultaneously.
Each element in this
an image of the All.

Chapter Seven

The Way of Beauty

THIS CHAPTER ARISES OUT OF A split I feel in my own experience, a split that runs like an earthquake fault through our entire culture. For my whole life, I have enjoyed both mysticism and art. Most of the world sees these as different realms; however, my direct experience says they are the same thing conceived under different terms. There is some religious art that links art and religion, but this is only a small overlap. Not surprisingly, we will have to dig into the experience of art to see where it connects to religion and mysticism. So, for a while, forget we are concerned with mysticism or religion. For the moment, we are in the realm of the beautiful.

The Experience of Art

What is art? I include all of the arts: painting, sculpture, music, literature, the decorative arts, architecture, etc. Actually, the realm is a good deal larger than this brief listing, for it includes anything that someone finds beautiful. Human beings themselves can be seen as art or as just people. For most people, the whole natural world is a form of beauty. Therefore, I define art as whatever someone finds beautiful. Out of all the things of existence, the realm of art encompasses those things one would like to have, to live with, and to enjoy repeatedly. In this chapter, I will refer particularly to paintings in my examples because they illustrate my points, but painting is used just to represent this wider realm. As a person who enjoys art, I don't feel any gap between the different forms of art. Somehow the same fundamental process underlies the enjoyment of it all.

Most texts on art treat it as an external object. They describe different paintings, music, or architecture as things that are "out there." They may be visual, as in the fine arts and literature, or aural, as in an opera or any musical composition. Art, in this standard context, is something that is outside of us and comes to us. However, I contend that, to really understand this realm, we must deal with art as perceived or experienced, as an internal experience. After all, a Rembrandt is great art to many, but to some it is boring, just painted old fogies. We have to get at the process that shifts the experience from dull, painted canvas to a moment to remember for a lifetime. For me, the experience of art is so simple that it surprises me that a large segment of the population hasn't figured out how to enjoy it. The foundation of art experience can be illustrated by a game I play with children in art galleries.

My seven-year-old grandson and I are in a gallery of paintings. For him this can easily become an experience just for adults, not for him. So, let us make it a game. We pretend that he can choose and take home any one of these paintings in each room. He goes around the room studying each. "Which one is yours?," I ask. He points to his choice. Often it is one with vivid colors. Or it may have a scene he can identify with. With his choice revealed, I stand and admire it approvingly. His choice is taken seriously because he is showing me something of *his* interior. He is too young for me to ask, "Why this one?" The answer would likely be, "I just like it." In a large museum, we go on with this exercise from room to room. There is an underlying assumption that he can find what he likes as well as any adult. When my wife and I enjoy this same game, we can reveal more of the basis of our choice. She surprised me once by choosing a small photograph of canned fruit on the dusty shelf of a shack. Here was her artistic domesticity.

What is involved in this simple exercise? As human beings, we experience many feelings and underlying currents. Certain of these we consistently enjoy. We are able to recognize any hint in the world of the most subtle representation of what we enjoy within. For example, I have purchased a series of paintings that at first look very different. One is a semiabstract mountain, another is the edge of a lake, another has whales swimming at the foot of a glacier. They look different, but all have the same mood. One of these illustrates this point, a small oil painting of a lake shore with a dock. The artist painted it at dusk in dark hues. It is a scene of utter peace and quiet. Serenity is the inner state I enjoy, so I recognized it in the painting. Hanging on the wall, this small painting helps bring me back to this state. So, I tend to collect as my own paintings that evoke a feeling of peace and serenity.

This is the initial opening into the world of art enjoyment. Find what the person easily finds pleasurable. Do you want to teach music appreciation? Find the music the person already enjoys. Start to explore its structure and composition. Then deal with similar and related kinds of music. Gradually, expand the range of music a person can enjoy. In all the arts, the more you know of the art the more the enjoyment you feel. In music, you need to hear the major theme and then look for its variations. Teaching art appreciation must be a delightful experience because you are expanding people's sphere of enjoyment. Art is really the artist's subtle inner experience gotten out and made available so others can find themselves in it. The process is one of continual discovery. Over and over, I have found that a work of art that first meant little to me could become significant. And with each discovery, I expand contact with and understand my inner self. With a house full of paintings chosen by me, I am there, at every turn, showing forth in varied and lovely forms. This isn't really a narcissistic process. For Narcissus to fall in love with his own image, he had to think it was someone else. No, I am there on the walls. The very fixedness of the paintings is satisfying. We are all constantly changing inwardly, so it is a bit of relief to find reminders of our meaningful inner passions steadily before us.

How do you get to finding your ideal state on the walls? You simply give the work of art some time. Open yourself up to its effects. Then, from your own inner reactions, you experience what the art can do to you. When you chose a work of art to live with, you chose an outer representation of your own ideal state. Art you want to live with really narrows the choices to the state you prefer. I consider this simple process the very foundation of the enjoyment of art. And after finding yourself in art, you then can go on and enjoy finding others in art.

I met the inner Rembrandt in the National Gallery in Washington, D.C. It was quite an experience. Of course, he died in 1669, but there on the walls was his carefully crafted expression of himself. Rembrandt was a portrait painter, but he drifted into what was more meaningful to him. He wanted to paint the very inside and nature of a person. This is no small feat to do in oil on a flat canvas. I remember the power of one painting of a wrinkled old woman, perhaps his mother, and a whole series of self-portraits done in different periods during his life. He reached his ideal. He captured the very nature of the person he painted, giving an entirely different dimension to portraiture. He must have experienced depth in himself to find the depth of others.

Vincent Van Gogh also impresses me. What I experience in his painting is a man on a passionate quest to express feeling and life.

Van Gogh was caught up to a wild extent in this process. The intensity he expressed in his self-portraits is nearly frightening, expressed mostly in his bold lines but partly in vivid colors. Most people think of a sunflower as a pretty little form. But Van Gogh's sunflowers are wild with passionate feeling. He lived in a barely controlled intensity of feeling, which shows everywhere in his art.

Now how can one meet the artist? Simply let the art affect you and interpret out of that personal feeling the other life that is shown in intimate detail before you. Poor artists express themselves poorly. Great artists stand out in bold and definite relief as unique as their art. Artists capture their own essence for others to see and enjoy. Of course, not all art comes across to the viewer so easily. Big canvases that are essentially just divided by two or three colors juxtaposed seemed just too simple to do much to me. However, I was once in a gallery with a man whom I considered rather shallow. Suddenly, he pointed across the room to one of these two-colored paintings and said, "Now that would do well in a dark corner." He was serious. Suddenly, I saw it too. Yes, that is where it would fit. It had a quiet, somber mood. He helped me to suddenly step from just two colors to the very mood and feeling of the work.

Art is really the highest and the best that people can get out of themselves, to present in a form for others to experience. For instance, Shaker furniture shows a whole concept of life. Feelings are broader than words, so my impression of life as portrayed in furniture is hard to describe. The Shaker life is very balanced, fine, and simple. They must be dignified and self-possessed people. Simple beauty. No frills or fancies. Very honest and open. These are the Shakers experienced in their lovely furniture.

This process of finding yourself and others in art has some deep lessons in it. We can't actually enjoy art unless there is a corresponding potential in ourselves, near the surface. If I can't feel, the art is just a silent thing. I must be open and sensitive to encounter it. We need all the outer representations we can get of ourselves and others. We are such mysterious creatures that we might never finish making discoveries in endless representations.

There is also a kind of mystery in the memory of art. It is as though whatever we love becomes a part of us. Rembrandt and Van Gogh are with me, burned into my memory. My life is enriched by them. Notice that I did not write "was enriched"; the experience of art is not transitory. What we really love remains with us eternally. And having our inner house full of these treasures, we are enriched. In some sense, we are what we have collected into our lives. It is best to throw out the trash and keep only what is worth keeping. I hope you see by now that art isn't just a thing out there. The experience of art reveals the inner in the outer.

Literature is an excellent example of a way to explore possible human worlds. Great literature deals sensitively with all the nuances of human experience and interactions. Drama presents the human in a tightly conceived story. Poetry presents these matters in a briefer and more imaginative and implicit way. Music captures more of the emotional tone and quality of the inner. We really need all the arts. For a moment, picture the world with all its great art gone. We would have lost all the inspiration of the past. It would be a far meaner and shallower world. Human potential would be lost. It would be much work to develop it all over again, and we probably could never capture art that reflects a particular people, time, and culture. African sculpture would be gone. We would never see the ivory triptychs of the Byzantine empire again. We would be far less without all these.

Many see art as just a pretty decorative addition to the world. But it is actually a broad range of representations of the highest human capabilities. We need these representations. The best work of many people reminds us of what is possible. Without art, we partly lose touch with all they capture and represent. A culture like Communism, which stresses all-functional, propagandistic art, starves the human. Communist art was hardly art at all because it was so limited to the state's purpose of selling its program. A study of Shostakovich's Symphony no. 10 shows how he suffered under

Communism and broke out in powerful self-expression when permitted. One marvelous aspect of art is the way each production is the result of another person's realizing his or her potential. Though we can teach art and expand artistic appreciation, I hardly feel we really understand all its deepest human uses. When forced to be away from art for a time, I can feel a palpable longing for something beautiful. Art seems to deal easily with the depths of human aspiration and feeling. We know hardly anything of this realm. But to anyone who has lived in art and enjoyed it, it seems as essential as life itself.

The Experience of Art and Mysticism

There is a point at which art and mysticism join. It is at the level of the human experience of both. We will look at the experience of each before joining them.

Although art is normally conceived as objects out there, here we are dealing with art as experience. It is then some sort of relationship between the perceiver and the perceived. Those who can enjoy art have the magic key to this relationship. In the broadest way, we first enjoy art that resonates with our own nature. In my basic exercise of getting either children or adults to find the piece in a gallery they most want, it is this resonating relationship that is involved. I mentioned that once in a gallery I chose a painting that was essentially just three horizontal bands of color. Normally I would reject such a painting. If it is so simple that I could do it, then it is not good enough! So why choose this over all other candidates? The three bands of color became a sandy beach with gray ocean beyond and sky on the horizon. I would enjoy living with this one because it has the same meditative mood I so enjoy. But why buy a painting to have my mood adjusted? On my wall, the painting gives me access to the experience I most want and enjoy. It is more than a reminder. It is the very way in. Comparing my everyday life of worldly involvements and the way of this painting, my ordinary life seems partly lost and scattered. But with this painting, it is suddenly gathered up and focused. The painting gives me access to my ideal, a vital function. Of course, I am using my own experience merely to illustrate a process available to everyone. In my art exercise, I have also asked of my wife's choice or that of any friend with me. If I have found mine, why do I want also to know other peoples? In a love relationship, friendships, and indeed in any acquaintance, I am simply curious to find how others are different.

To me this is the second great function of art. On the simplest level, I find my own center. But in asking others of their experience, I am shown other worlds. Some people's worlds are so covered over, it is terribly difficult to get even a dim glimpse. My sister is one of these. We mostly fought through childhood. So years later, when I discovered her interest in Zen mysticism, I thought that we should be able to have a wonderful dialogue. Not in the least. She is ready to speak of everyone but herself. The other day I received a postcard from her. In the blank upper corner of its address side she drew a lovely still life in colored pencil. I had to examine it under a magnifying glass to convince myself that she was giving me only the second piece of art I ever got from her. On the back part, she finally spoke as a mystic: "The absolute is simply everything in our world emptied of personal emotional content— or the recipe for living is simply to do what we are doing." There, in a few lines, I finally understood her. Her mysticism is simpler than mine. She lives in this absolute, emptied of personal content. No wonder it is hard to get to know her as a person. She also insisted I read *Nothing Special* by a Zen teacher, a book I promptly ordered.[1] Though on the surface my sister seemed to have slapped my wrist, I felt absolutely delighted. I thanked her for her card and put it in my life mementos. When the Absolute speaks to me, I pay attention.

This incident illustrates the second great use of art. It goes

---

1. Charlotte Joko Beck, *Nothing Special* (San Francisco: Harper, 1993).

beyond self-discovery into the lives of others. I particularly like to see happy, well-ordered lives, perhaps designed along principles I have never known before. When I enjoy animals and plants, I have much the same feeling. Here is a lovely, well-ordered life structure along lines I barely grasp. The experience is broadening. It is a natural way to learn tolerance and patience. I fully expect heaven to show me ever more of the wonder of other lives.

But now and then I meet lives in such disorder that they are opposite of this ideal. I once did business with a woman who lived in a rural setting. One time I had to see her and found the place around her home a total junkyard and garbage heap. I knocked and couldn't raise her and finally walked in the open door. The house was little trails through a mix of heaps of things and garbage. Those who deal with quantities of garbage will know its universal smell. She frightened me when suddenly she arose out of a heap of rubbish I took to be her bed. Besides our financial dealings, she wanted to ask me a business question. Her quite mistaken impression was that I was a clever businessman. Her question was, "Would I do well opening a shop to sell Bibles in the nearest small town?" The question was easy. I suggested she would probably lose money on a Bible store. But here was a life that was appalling.

What do we learn from other lives? What is possible. In a way lives seem like art objects. They show forth their design. They say, "Look, this is possible, too." Art and people's lives look like the endless playful creativity of a God who does it so easily. Even my garbage friend shows this is possible too. People can so lose themselves as to merge with garbage.

But we have now come down to the essence of art as an experience. On one level, through the leading of our own enjoyment, it directs us to our personal center, what we really are and would choose to be eternally. But beyond this, art opens us to the richness of other lives. It is not by accident that I have mixed art, people's lives, and even the natural beauty of animal and plant lives. In some ways, others' lives enrich mine, and mine hopefully enriches theirs. It is a shared world with enough to go around for all. Even my garbage lady, and all the other lost souls, are part of this richness. Their lives say, "You could miss out, too." By contrast this makes any finding a most welcome success.

Now let us look at religion as a process. A friend, though born a Christian, converted to Judaism. He remarked that Judaism leads to high holy moments that Jews rarely refer to. I suddenly realized that this is characteristic of all religions. There is some kind of tacit conspiracy of silence about high holy moments. Buddhists rarely even hint at them for fear that any presumption will destroy these illuminations. These high holy moments become clearer in saints who enjoy such moments so constantly that the news gets out, and people are attracted to these mystics.

What then takes place in these transcending experiences in which religion really lives? The person and his or her situation fuse in a kind of resonating relationship. There is no longer an "I" among things, but things and I come alive with meaning and portent. It is tremendously enjoyable. Once, while driving, I noticed how different kinds of trees found their proper place in relation to a stream. On the banks of the river were trees with lacy branches, while further back were firs. Then suddenly it was as though the cosmos were speaking and instructing me. "Of course, all life manages to find its place." In these transcendent moments we find our place, and the world seems to come alive and show forth its nature. And in the process I and it are the same. Duality dissolves, and there is a flood of meaning/enjoyment.

If I went on with more examples, it would become apparent that the experience of art and the experience of God are much the same. Given a set of circumstances, we remain open and receptive. The situation comes alive with meaning/enjoyment. I put meaning and enjoyment together this way because sometimes one predominates and sometimes the other. Not all meaning can be defined, and then it is mystery. But there is always the sense of the enjoyment of Life present. Life comes forth and reveals itself.

At this level of experience, I find it difficult to tell the difference between the experience of beauty in art or God. There is the matter of the name. One is, of course, of God and the other of beauty. But in the experience itself, God/Love/Beauty are one. Also there is no dualism of me-versus-it. If you look at art dualistically, as if it were an "other" outside of yourself, you ruin it. You think, "What am I supposed to see here?" You are supposed to see whatever arises for you. For those who get hung up on the name "God," I would like to hand them a big heavy dictionary giving all the names of God in all cultures and times. Among them would surely be Wonder, Awe, Love, Beauty, and others like these. And these are the names of art also.

I warrant that if we compare formal religion and art they seem rather different in their forms. And when we examine how they serve us, art is, to my mind, vastly the superior. Just note the predilection of religion for doctrine that leads to endless human debate. Compare this to a Rembrandt or a Van Gogh that wordlessly ushers us into a world of beauty. We surely need more art and less argument and killing over doctrine.

But I grant a kind of intrinsic difficulty in finding the experience of God and art as the same. You, the real percipient, need to move freely in both realms for some while to come to see them as intrinsically the same process. If you insist on tallying up differences, however, then it seems to me art is, hands down, superior. Perhaps you never expected a dyed-in-the-wool mystic like me to come out with the superiority of art. But there it is.

Training Mystics

Were I to have the task of training mystics, I would use the way of art appreciation as the easiest and most pleasant entrance into the field. With no discussion of God or religion whatever, a person can begin directly on the basic mind set that leads to mystical experience. Through this avenue, you could as well work with people who have that common negativity to anything that smacks of religion. You know the kind I mean: mention God and religion and you instantly see a glaze form over their eyes. Religion is, at the least, frightfully dull to them, but in addition, they may have an aversion to it. Such people live at a great distance from the entrance into the mystical. But often these same people are open to learning how to experience beauty. If I had a number of people to train, of all ages (including children), I would like to divide them into small working groups, preferably under twenty. Young people might do better in groups closer their age. If possible, I would also begin where each was, in the art form they already most enjoy. To create mystics, I could work in any of the arts.

The basic pattern of training would be to start at an appropriate level for each person and with the art form that is right for each. For example, a teenager might be more drawn to music than to sculpture. Then use the standard means of art appreciation to move into the appreciation of a widening variety of forms of their art. Somewhere along the line, we would speak about our individual feelings. Each would set about to discover the central mood or feeling that he or she would most enjoy. We could also discuss questions such as what is real harmony in living—always having the art medium as a form to refer to. When students have discovered their own nature and center and the harmony they most enjoy, they will have arrived at the entrance to mystical experience. At this entrance, I would then ask them to create forms in their art they enjoy. They would derive this out of themselves. Whether they produced great art in any outward sense would not matter. Its value would be in relation to *what is most meaningful to them.* When they create what is meaningful to them, they will have crossed from the threshold of the mystical into the very home of it. As they explore either in their creations or in the creations of others, they would be in the field of mystical experience. One day, if it had not happened already, they would use this whole way of art appreciation to feel moved by life itself. These are experiences in which one feels led into meaning experiences larger than one's self. This *is* mystical experience, whether or not it has labels of

God or religion on it. They would be inclined to go on enjoying the experience of leaving themselves open to learning from what transcends them. I can see their personal expressions of this capacity being presented in various ways. It could be in the fine arts, or in writing, or they could turn philosophical. These experiences might be used solely for guidance in their life, with no outer expression to others. In short, the experience could be used in a variety of ways, few of which might have a God label. My sister seems to use what she is given for personal guidance, with practically no outer expression for others. Obviously, the guidance I receive is almost immediately put in writing and eventually made available for others to use as they will. Various outcomes are possible.

And one central point I would make. Though such people are beginning mystics, only a small proportion of them may finally link this experience to the "perennial philosophy" of religion. If trainees in this system were already practicing members of a faith, then I would expect at some point that they would report, to their great surprise, that their art appreciation had made them see deeper into their own faith. I have met many such people. They have heard standard passages from the Bible since childhood, but suddenly the same passage acquired a depth of meaning. It is pleasant for something to open into significance.

Perhaps this connection between art appreciation and mystical experience would make more sense if I put it into sequence. Through art appreciation, it is simply fun to learn that what you had been treating in a limited way can gradually open out to a great richness. It is a combination of learning more details of the art and allowing yourself to experience a greater range of it. At first it seems you are learning the art—perhaps how to use watercolors or how to mold in clay or how to write a haiku—but it gradually becomes apparent that you are also learning to experience. When you find through art your own central tendencies, you have come to the threshold of the mystical. It is in your own central tendencies that you are gripped by life itself. A major turning point into the mystical has arrived when the same approach to art leads into seeing into the meaning of life itself. It is very like studying painting and suddenly realizing your life is a massive painting in itself. In art you are dealing with a beauty that transcends you, from which you can respectfully learn. In this pleasurable exploration, you wander from what speaks to you of your small life to beginning to learn of life itself. So the sequence is:

(1) learn of art
(2) learn of yourself in relation to art
(3) learn of your own center and nature
(4) pursue your life tendencies to life itself.

In an ideal society, this sequence would be a part of a basic education for everyone. I see it as basic because, knowing this lesson, you can always find your center again and life itself, no matter how bad things get.

Thus, training in art can be used as the avenue into mystical experience because, quite simply, they are part of the same process. Art looks different in its materials; but the more it is seen as a process involving us, the more apparent is its connection to mystical experience.

It would be pleasant to live in a world in which everyone were put through the training described above early in life, with periodic reinforcement and development, all the way to adulthood. Ideally, I would like to see a world in which art is rampant, where everyone is beautifying in his or her own way. The possible forms would enrich and vary far more than we see today. Artistic ability would be noted and supported. Great artists would have influence something as statesmen have today. All old forms of art would be cared for and made available to everyone. And tolerance would reign in a world in which each had found his or her own nature and understood how it fits into the rich variety of our differences. And here and there, in some lovely garden, there would be serious discussions of what all this means for those who must put words to it. And one of the mystics would say, "It means simply we are in the midst of God's endless creativity."

This quotation comes from the essay "Beauty" by the Greek mystic Plotinus, written in the second century CE. Plotinus is in the beauty/God realm:

> *Anyone who has seen it knows what I mean, in what sense it is beautiful. As good, it is desired and towards it desire advances. But only those reach it who rise to the intelligible realm, face it fully, stripped of the muddy vesture with which they were clothed in their descent (just as those who mount to the temple sanctuaries must purify themselves and leave aside their old clothing), and enter in nakedness, having cast off in the ascent all that is alien to the divine. There one, in the solitude of self, beholds simplicity and purity, the existent upon which all depends, towards which all look, by which reality is, life is, thought is. For the Good is the cause of life, of thought, of being.*
>
> *Seeing, with what love and desire for union one is seized—what wondering delight! If a person who has never seen this hungers for it as for his all, one that has seen it must love and reverence it as authentic beauty, must be flooded with an awesome happiness, stricken by a salutary terror. Such a one loves with a true love, with desires that flame.[2]*

The following, on Tibetan sacred art, comes from a contemporary Buddhist work. It refers to Tibetan Buddhist *thankas*, which are artistic representations of enlightenment. They are used by Buddhists as art that reflects the qualities of enlightenment which the perceiver may approach by meditating on the *thanka*.

> *The purpose of traditional Buddhist art is to express the indescribable beauty of the Buddha's enlightened qualities so that they remain deeply imprinted in our memory. Each*

---

2. Plotinus, *The Essential Plotinus*, trans. Elmer Green (New York: New American Library, 1964).

color and shape is a significant symbol, explained in the texts. Observing the forms and considering their meanings move us beyond merely thinking about beauty toward contemplation of beauty.

Joined with contemplation, love of beauty can guide us through the darkness of our lives. As the senses respond to aesthetic form, they become gateways for the light of Buddha's realization to enter into our being, transforming the mind and purifying the heart. Our way of seeing begins to merge with our way of being, and we find ourselves in a heavenly paradise.[3]

The appreciation of art is the entrance into all that is higher in life. God is all things of good. The beautiful is good embodied.

---

3. Yeshe De Project, ed. *The Art of Enlightenment* (Berkeley, Calif.: Dharma Publishing, 1985).

Chapter Eight

Gazing at the Spiritual in an Icon[1]

S PIRITUAL PRACTICE IS A SIM-
ple way of getting into the spiritual. Commonly known practices
include meditation, breathing exercises, and the repetition of a
mantra. In this chapter, I take an icon of the Eastern Orthodox
Church and discover a highly successful form of spiritual practice.
But those outside of this church may need a little introduction to
icons.

The Eastern Orthodox Church is a mystical church in which
the experience of God is sought. This church has a tradition of
using icons, dating back to the earliest days of Christianity. It was
said that the Apostle Luke painted icons. Such figures date further
back to Egyptian tomb paintings, which attempted a realistic

---

1. This chapter first appeared as "Spiritual Practice with an Icon," *Sacred Art Journal* 12, no. 1
(March 1991): 3–10; and is reprinted by permission.

portrait of the deceased. In the Orthodox Church, icons are religious paintings of Christ, the Virgin, the Apostles and saints, and scenes from the Bible. Over the centuries since the dawn of Christianity, people would commission the creation of an icon in paint, mosaic, or other materials. The aim was to create a window into the spiritual. The lover of icons learns to see through the representation into the spiritual. The centuries-long selection process led to traditions as to the style that works best for the perceiver. For the Orthodox, in a church with walls covered with icons, it is quite like being in the midst of a heavenly host, alive, present, and gazing down on the worshipers.

In the 700s CE, the Church went through a disruptive iconoclastic controversy. Some felt that the Orthodox were idolizing the icons, a ridiculous charge to one who has learned to see through the spiritual window of the icon. The iconoclasts, bent on destroying the images, seem not to have learned how to see the spiritual through an icon. So, it looked to them as though the people worshiping a painting or other representation were engaged in idolatry.

My own icon is a thirty-cent reproduction on cardboard. I have no doubt it is just a picture on cardboard, nothing special. I even bought thirty of them, so I could teach others. The worshiper, seeking the spiritual, can find it through the instrument of this representation. The picture is like a window you learn to see through. You can see the spiritual without it, but when you join the throng using icons stretching back through the centuries, the representation is a help.

Over the centuries, icons were shaped and reshaped to be effective windows into the spiritual. The saint or figure in this art looks right at the perceiver in a kind of spiritual confrontation. His or her expression is serious because it is life and death, the meaning of life, and your salvation that are involved. There are a great many symbols and signs in this art. One subtle aspect is that icons are done in reverse perspective. Instead of the edges of a Bible held by a saint retreating in the distance, it is as though the

Bible comes forward, reaching out to the viewer. In contrast to the stylized seriousness of Orthodox icons, Western religious art tends to be pretty, almost like Valentine Day cards.

Seeing through the icon window into the spiritual has everything to do with who you are and what you are attempting to do. It is far from idolizing wood and paint. It is an interaction of a form, an ancient tradition, and the spirituality of the perceiver. With a little study of the traditional form of icons, I found that they came alive for me. Out of curiosity, I simply set out to see what steadily gazing at my favorite icon for fifteen minutes per day could do. I worked through various difficulties and came into one of the greatest experiences of my life. A useful spiritual practice emerged. When I checked with Church authorities, none knew of icon-gazing as a spiritual practice. But I concluded that I had only rediscovered what saints like St. Seraphim of Sarov surely already knew. Here follows my formal report to the Orthodox, to reintroduce what I believe to be an ancient way. There are contemporary Hindus and Buddhists who recognized this spiritual practice as quite like their own.

It appears to me that I have rediscovered an ancient way of working with icons. I will describe the method in sufficient detail so that others may try it. After that, I will give my reasons for believing that this is a rediscovery rather than a new development. Basically, the method involves selecting a single icon and turning to it daily for spiritual comfort and guidance. It is the long-term daily work for a year or more with a single icon that sets this method apart from the conventional uses of icons. It is a method in itself, just as the *Jesus Prayer* is a method, which has been described many times and passed from one to another as a useful approach.

My own background made it particularly likely for me to rediscover this approach. I am a clinical psychologist who has worked for some decades in the area between psychology and religion. My work is concerned with method. Even in reading the lives of saints, I am inclined to ask practical questions such as, "How did they proceed?" and "What did they find?" I have learned that, in their almost heroic struggles, the early Church Fathers made many discoveries, some of which are little known today; their writings about these spiritual discoveries lie covered beneath the sands of time. I have yet to find anyone else who knows of the method I am about to describe; I hope not only to make it available for others' use, but also to encourage the response of others who may know of it. Its basic thrust—long-term spiritual work with a single icon—is so obvious that I simply cannot believe it is totally unknown. I have deliberately explored the parameters of the method in order to be able to describe it to others. I am quite aware of individual differences in spiritual experience, but my impression is that spiritual methods are rather like theme and variation in music. I will attempt to describe the basic parameters of the method (the theme), using some of my own personal experiences (variations) only to illustrate these parameters.

Long-Term Work with an Icon

The first step is to choose an icon to which you feel attracted. It can be mounted or unmounted, hand-painted or a reproduction. I have heard some say that an icon must be blessed, but this too is unnecessary. My own icon, as I've already noted, cost me thirty cents and is postcard-sized. I did paste it to cardboard to make it more substantial. The reason I suggest choosing one you are attracted to is that there is already a link between the icon and yourself, although you need not know why this link exists. The icon can be of a single figure, several figures, or a scene. These differences are not critical. But I do recommend icons in the Byzantine tradition rather than Westernized religious pictures. Why? As you become deeply involved with icons, you will begin to feel the difference. Westernized religious pictures seem superficial, made pretty, like advertisements. Icons in the Byzantine tradition seem much more solidly spiritual.

I have read a good deal on icons; often scholars stress that they follow tradition. In fact, the tradition has been described.[2] Some people come to the conclusion that the Church dogmatically set what was acceptable, and this became tradition. What I honestly believe happened is that people's choices over the centuries gradually set tradition. People bought and commissioned icons, and this choice was based on what personally felt right for them. I believe the Byzantine icon tradition is the outcome of centuries of personal choices as to what worked for individuals. The use of icons was more serious in the Byzantine tradition than in the West and quite beyond religious decoration. It attempted to picture the spiritual itself, and people's choices reflected what they felt worked towards this end. Thus, I recommend choosing an icon in the Byzantine tradition.

Having chosen an icon, you should then simply gaze at it for a minimum of ten minutes per day, or as often as convenient. I quickly learned to enjoy the process, and my time rose to an average nearer twenty-seven minutes, with individual sessions lasting up to one hour. I discovered that the process was so timeless that I would have difficulty knowing if a session were five minutes long or thirty, so I took to timing sessions with a stopwatch. Why time the timeless? For one thing, I was trying to understand a method and needed the data, but also it helped orient me in a process that was more timeless than I was accustomed to. I would say timing is a matter of personal choice, and likely the ancients did not do it, simply because watches were not yet invented.

I also learned to keep a pad and pencil handy. While gazing at the icons, sudden subtle insights would come to me. I chose to write these down to help fix them, so they would not be lost. I now have enough insights to do a book on the subject. This too is a matter of choice, and one the ancients are unlikely to have done; but I recommend it. In part, writing down your insights reflects respect for what was given to you. I recommend working with

---

2. Constantine Kalokyris, *Orthodox Iconography* (Brookline, Mass.: Holy Cross Orthodox Press, 1985).

your icon when you are unlikely to be disturbed and are not too tired. Once you get into the process, you could do it almost any time anywhere. As an experiment, I have had productive sessions with the television on. I mention this just to suggest how substantial the process can become. Especially in the early stages, one needs quiet isolation. Now, if the telephone rings or I am called to other duties, I have no difficulty shifting to them.

These, then, are the bare externals of the situation: a Byzantine icon of your choice, gazed at ten minutes or longer per day, in a state of quiet isolation. You might choose to time sessions and to note down your findings.

Now let us turn to the inner attitude. Basically, like the early Fathers, I assume that the icon is a window that opens out on the spiritual. I assume it is likely that I might learn from the spiritual. You need not do anything but gaze and remain open to experiencing. You are looking at the spiritual. Simply be open to whatever comes; there is no special state to strive for beyond this. If the spiritual were before you, would you not simply look with reverence? There is already a great deal implied in this simple approach. For one, the experience of gazing at the spiritual is peaceful and relaxing. I have noticed my heartbeat and respiration dropping rapidly as I enter this peaceful spiritual place. I have questioned whether or not any picture might do or even any point of concentration. When in the midst of work with my icon, I have tried shifting to other icons. It was my impression that I would have to start all over with months of work to get to where I was with my familiar icon. And other kinds of pictures simply do not anchor one in the spiritual. With them, you can drift off to anything. The fact that the icon was created out of centuries-long spiritual effort helps to anchor and hold one in the spiritual. The early Fathers remarked that one can learn from cave walls. I agree, but they were already quite advanced when they turned to cave walls. This is similar to fixing attention on any point in Zen Buddhist meditation. For a person starting out, I recommend the spiritual anchor of a Byzantine icon.

Early Stages of Icon Work

I would like to distinguish what is learned in the beginning from what takes place later, in more mature stages. In the beginning, one is probably not accustomed to seeing the spiritual, especially in the form of a static picture. So the beginning stages are like a series of little discoveries. For one, I would recommend learning whatever you can about your icon, with a special emphasis on the story of the figure(s) represented. Do not be surprised if you can learn next to nothing, other than what is represented. I studied the language of iconography: how the artist shaped the picture to represent the spiritual. Some of this is known, but most of it has been forgotten. For instance, it is not essential that a saint's icon look like the physical saint. It is the spirituality of the saint that is represented rather than his or her appearance. I was pleased to learn, for instance, that the Bible shown being held in my icon is painted in traditional reversed perspective (as I mentioned earlier, as though it comes out toward the viewer rather than retreating). But if you can find out little about your icon, do not be concerned. The process will instruct you.

In the early stages, I wandered from detail to detail and tried to understand each. I would feel drawn to a detail and would dwell on it until a satisfactory meaning came to me. Some of these meanings hit me with great impact and certainty. I will give an example. My icon is labeled "St. Innocent of Irkutsk." One would assume that one is dealing with a specific person. In my icon, he has a ragged beard and hair and a thin drawn face as befits a saint who labored long and hard in the icy tundra of Siberia. Yet it came to me one day that I was seeing not *this man* but the spiritual itself. That is, he had worked long and hard toward the spiritual, and now the spiritual itself was showing, not the person. This was signaled by many aspects in the icon, including the Bible, cross, robes, crown, and halo. This is the implication of a saint, a person in whom the spiritual shows through.

I will give another discovery to illustrate this early stage.

During one session, I felt drawn to the odd feature that his hands were far younger than the rest of him. Instead of assuming that the artist made a mistake (which is to go to the external), I turned to the spirituality of the icon to show me what this meant. I saw that one hand holds a Bible, and the other a cross. Then it came to me. What he is holding is forever new (i.e., youthful), and this was represented by young hands. Whenever you come to an aspect in your icon work that puzzles you, turn to the spiritual itself to instruct you, and be patient. Let the answer come to you while you are anchored in the spiritual. In this way, the early part of the icon work is a gradual accumulation of spiritual discoveries and meanings.

Early on I was bothered that, though individual elements had meaning, I could not pull it all together into a single picture. Then, one day, it did all come together, focused in the eyes of the saint. Everything revealed a single spirituality. I later tried shifting to other icons as an experiment. Though my ability to feel other icons had deepened, I had accumulated so many insights of my own that I would have to start all over with another. My icon was like home and family, so familiar. Each of my discoveries had added to its meaning.

When it comes all together in a single spiritual presence, you have entered into the more mature stages.

Mature Work with an Icon

In the early stages, the icon grows in importance, until it comes together as a spiritual experience. It is as though you have found a quiet, pleasant chapel you can visit any time. You become accustomed to returning to its peace and respite. Along the way, you learn the spiritual is ready to answer your deepest questions and concerns. A major aspect of the more mature work with an icon comes about simply because you have grown accustomed to working with the spiritual. Again, let me illustrate with an insight. In general, the icon experience is quite lively, but I would occasionally have sessions in which there was nothing to write down, as though nothing had happened. After some further work, I discovered what these meant. I was expecting something clear and obvious. But I was being *reformed* by a process that was more subtle and comprehensive than my limited expectations. I learned that these apparently empty sessions were full in an unexpected way: personal reformation was underway. This is what I meant by the process being more subtle and comprehensive than I expected.

In case some might think this icon work would be boring, let me point out a simple fact. I frequently find looking at the eyes of my saint too intense or immediate an experience, and so turn to some other peripheral detail in order to lessen the intensity.

As I worked with my icon, I felt a great interest in certain aspects of the teaching of the early Fathers. I searched in the *Philokalia,* and wrote down every quote on watchfulness, silence, the heart center, and the Holy Spirit.[3] I now strongly recommend that others do the same, especially in the more mature stages of icon work. I have several reasons for this. The most important one is that, in the advanced stages of this practice, the teachings of the early Fathers in these matters go directly to the central aspect of what is happening. They are so absolutely relevant that this is one of the reasons I came to believe I was rediscovering what others had known before. Such a study at this point also provides another anchor in tradition. This icon method elaborates tradition, and tradition elaborates this method. Tradition has a particular bearing on the subtle aspects of icon work, greatly clarifying the nature of the process. It was a great comfort to discover that my findings paralleled those of the early Fathers.

I am reluctant to say too much about the more mature stages of this process. My feelings in this matter may be quite similar to those who went before but did not describe the process. It is as though one goes to consult the spiritual without really knowing

---

3. The *Philokalia* is an excellent collection of the work of spiritual masters in the Christian Orthodox tradition from the fourth to the fifteenth century. Saints Nikodimos and Markarios, *The Philokalia,* 4 vols. (Boston: Faber and Faber, 1979–1983).

what to expect. The early Fathers' teachings on watchfulness, silence, and the heart center go directly to how to approach the spiritual. The early Fathers say repeatedly that one should have few words and no imagery. An analogy would be a serious conversation with a friend. If you have too much to say, you do not learn of your friend's situation. Imagery is similar. If you have too many images or preconceptions, you are filled with expectations and cannot see what is being shown to you. In watchful silence, you are wide open and ready to receive anything. You certainly can pray to the icon, but it should be with the knowledge that the spiritual knows your concerns better than you. You might then briefly phrase them just so you can hear them. The icon is a method of silence *par excellence.* And your silence leaves you open and ready to learn.

The teachings on the heart center are even more pertinent. In our materialistic way, we have come to think of the heart center as the physical location of the heart. The early Fathers were really speaking of the center of your concerns and the source of your life. These deep concerns are given to you. You can always enter interaction with the spiritual through your heart center, that is, your deepest concerns. You can always approach the icon through the heart center because it is the very source of your life and your understanding. In the heart center are both the Holy Spirit and your own deepest aspects. In this center, your life and the spiritual meet and interact. This provides the spiritual searcher a central key. You can surely find your deepest concerns, and they are the way to the Holy Spirit. As St. Diadochos of Photiki writes, "He who dwells . . . within his own heart . . . lives in the Spirit. . . ."[4]

Dwelling in the heart is to be aware of your deepest concerns beyond words and images, silently, aware that it is your own channel of communication with the Spirit. And the Spirit responds. As St. Hesychios the Priest writes, "A heart that has been completely

---

4. Ibid, vol. 1, 270, paragraph 57.

emptied of mental images gives birth to divine, mysterious intellections that sport within it like fish and dolphins in a calm sea. The sea is fanned by a soft wind, the heart's depth by the Holy Spirit."[5] It would be difficult to find a better description of the mature icon experience. I could easily multiply quotes and elaborate how they describe the later aspects of this approach. Watchful silence is the first key because you remain open and receptive. The heart center gives you a content with which to approach the spiritual. And finally, the icon work opens up contact with the Holy Spirit, which is also the God within, the Counselor. And this is the essence of icon work and of religion itself. I believe what the early Fathers affirmed—that contact with the Spirit is the whole point of religion.

I will not say too much of the mature side of icon work. This is enough to get someone started. It would be too much for a chapter. Once you become accustomed to working with the spiritual, you will have all the guidance you need.

It might help if I step back and simply react to this method. I would be hard put to find anything simpler than working a few minutes a day with a thirty-cent icon. But though simple to describe, this experience is quite the most surprising, unexpected, and enriching experience I have ever known. It contrasts greatly with all of the heavy tomes I have on theology. After a wide exploration with spiritual and psychological methods, this is my way of choice. I am particularly impressed with the way it works on many levels, gradually reforming my outlook and life in a wisely spiritual direction.

Rediscovery of a Method?

I am quite sure that icon-gazing a spiritual method because I am using it. The issue, then, is whether this icon-gazing is my own

---

5. Ibid, vol. 1, 190, paragraph 156.

discovery or whether others have discovered it before me. I began my investigation by asking everyone I knew in the Eastern Orthodox realm—laity, deacons, priests, monks—whether they had ever heard of long-term work with a single icon as a method in itself. All said no. Finally I wrote the eminent authority Constantine Cavarnos and received the same answer.[6] From these responses, I conclude that this meditative practice is little known—if not unknown—in the Eastern Orthodox literature.

That I am a special genius who found what generations of the Orthodox failed to find hardly seems likely to me. But I can see a number of reasons that this method might be more-or-less rediscovered repeatedly and yet not explicitly described. As a method, icon-gazing contrasts with the *Jesus Prayer*, which requires one to do something continuously. Also, the outsider is likely to fail to see the power of the *Jesus Prayer*. So someone more experienced needs to suggest this practice to the less experienced. This icon method does not require one to do anything special, except to spend regular time with an icon. A monk with an icon in his cell might spontaneously find this approach. But it might not appear to be a separate method since it was just another part of his whole religious life.

Also, we are in an age that questions methods. How-to books abound now. I first read the works of saints, hoping to learn precisely what they did and what developed thereby. Instead, for the most part, saints give one general doctrine with little or no reference to what they did. I gained more from sensitive biographers who followed the saint around and described what he or she was observed to do. So, even if this particular practice appeared to be a powerful approach to a saint, we are not likely to learn of it. Even the biographer would make little comment, except to say that saint so-and-so frequently prayed to his or her icon, which indeed was reported many times.

There is another subtle aspect. I found myself quite ready to

---

6. A personal letter dated January 17, 1990.

describe all of the opening aspects of this practice, but was reluctant to describe its deeper aspects. The early Fathers, being noted for greater humility, would be even more reluctant. Why the reluctance? For one thing, I would need the scope of a book. For another, the process is quite subtle and pervasive. It tends to reform the person, and I would have to spell out my idiocies that require reform. But finally, once a person finds a simple way into the presence of the Spirit, he or she does not need any further help from me. The Counselor leads from there.

I have dealt with a process that may be relatively common. Henri Nouwen's description of what he gained by some days alone with an icon comes close.[7] John Baggley's sensitive description is also noteworthy.[8] Whenever an individual comes to find comfort in frequent contact with a single icon, he or she is within the scope of this method. My guess is that one would begin by praying silently to an icon, then gradually learn to enjoy the richness of a silent relationship—and thus would have entered upon this approach. I believe there are thousands "out there" who have come to this. In my own way, I may have simply given form to what many others have also found. I cannot believe that millions of seekers working with icons over the centuries could fail to find it. For instance, I think of a particular icon of St. Seraphim of Sarov, which shows scenes of his life working with an icon of the Theotokos from childhood to old age. It is reported that he spent a considerable amount of time praying before this icon. I would assume that people like him knew of this use of icons. Also, this method fits so well with the most subtle teachings of the early Fathers as to suggest that some of them practiced it.

I have thought of one further possibility. If any other religion created religious pictures that were used in a similar way over a long term, it would be another kind of confirmation that others

---

7. Henri Nouwen, *Behold the Lord* (Notre Dame, In.: Ave Maria Press, 1978).

8. John Baggley, *Doors of Perception* (Crestwood, New York: St. Vladimir's Seminary Press, 1988).

found this possible. And, indeed, both Buddhist and Hindus work with *mandalas.* These are pictures that evolved over a long period of time to depict spiritual realities. Their use is much as I have described above. There are even some signs that they, too, have partly lost their own tradition. I have some Hindu descriptions of work with *mandalas* that are so convoluted I have to believe the author knows remarkably little of the actual practice. But, on the other hand, I have a description by a Tibetan Buddhist that is so perceptive that I believe he engaged in the actual practice.[9] Stylistically the *mandalas* are quite different from icons, but it appears to me that the basic intent (to picture the spiritual) and method are the same. The only apparent difference I can see is that a different religious tradition evolved a different way of picturing the spiritual.

I feel that there is a great use for icons here. Although I recognize that it is little known, I have to assume that it was discovered before by many, particularly since other religions have a similar practice. I would like to hear from anyone else who found it or who knows of references to it in any language. It seems sad to me that something so precious has been lost sight of over the centuries, so I felt I should speak up. A method needs a name, so I suggest this method be called "Gazing at the Spiritual."

---

9. Tarthang Tulku, *Sacred Art of Tibet* (Berkeley, Calif.: Dharma Publishing, 1974).

Chapter Nine

The Landscape of World Mysticism

FOR SOME YEARS, I HAVE SURveyed the world's literature on mysticism. After all, this is my major field; I should have at least a general understanding of it. I examined works of any and all religious traditions. Since youth, I had been collecting books in this area, but now I looked more seriously at the whole field.

I began with the general feeling that mystics are more alike than different, even though they come from different traditions. Although I ended up still feeling that mystics provide us with a universal message, the different traditions took on different attributes, as though I were beginning to distinguish individuals in a group. I knew the Western Christian mystic Emanuel Swedenborg quite early. I came out of this survey with a renewed appreciation for Swedenborg's work, so much so that I close this survey by coming back to the uniqueness of his contribution. I had not expected that I would discern individual differences and that my favorite in the beginning would be so enhanced by a survey of the whole.

This is a *personal* survey by a mystic of the landscape of the world's major mystical traditions. Because all my spiritual experiences have been of the universal rather than the sectarian, it is easy for me to look sympathetically at varied mystical traditions. The mystic is given such profound experiences that these color the whole life and outlook. It is not like having a body of academic training. The effects on the mystic are more on his or her feelings and how that person approaches the world. When I read mystics of other traditions, I look for indications that we have known similar experiences. This determination can be so acute that I see it in a single phrase or sentence. It doesn't require a lot of words or proofs. It can easily be seen even in a Zen garden design, a Buddhist *thanka*, or a Hindu mandala, so it can be verbal or nonverbal. The art of Zen embodies mystical experience, so if you have had that experience, it is recognizable. This is a key: you must have had the experience to recognize it in another. Yet, in spite of this, sometimes people of no great experience have a rather natural recognition because they already tend to be a mystic.

Do the varied forms in the different religions create a barrier? Not for long. These are temporary impediments, fairly easily overcome. Even though born in a Christian culture, I first recognized Zen Buddhism and then Hinduism. Christian mysticism was difficult until I ran into the Eastern Orthodox Church, which is a mystical Christian Church. Plotinus, a Greek pagan of 200 CE, was very easy to recognize from the first few lines of his works.

One other area of confusion needs to be dealt with. There are many in the occult (a word that means "dark" or "hidden") and esoteric traditions who pretend to be mystics. What gives them away is their general air of great secrecy and mystery, as though only they have found the way. Often they dangle some sort of carrot for you to pursue. For only $500, you can advance to the next level toward enlightenment.

On the other hand, true mystics as a group try to show the way freely. There are no secrets. But there are things you literally cannot grasp until your experience is greater. It would be interesting to do a book on fake mystics, including the one so wonderful that the way to enlightenment is to gaze on endless photos of him. This particular man also calls himself God. There is a bit of ego here that is totally uncharacteristic of mysticism. The experience of God creates humility. When you are receiving guidance from God, it is a serious error to mix it with your own speculations. Swedenborg and other mystics have been forbidden by God from any occult speculation. There is nothing mysterious, secret, occult, esoteric, or exclusive in mysticism, and any suggestion of these qualities indicates that the practice being described is not mysticism. Mysticism is essentially simple and democratic; it is for all people, everywhere. The viewpoint in mysticism is unusual to some simply because they have not explored the territory.

In surveying the entire landscape of world mysticism, it became necessary to describe hills and valleys, the high and the low, the light and dark. Otherwise I would end up saying all mystical traditions are equal, and the differences would not be so apparent. However, you can assume all in this survey are genuine mystics.

I understand that many readers would prefer to learn some biographical information on various mystics. However, I have not chosen that route because I do not want to suggest that the ones named are "the best." Here and there, I have reluctantly mentioned a few names, even though there are so many worthy representatives. My choice of example in these instances just means that I ran across this particular person while reading a text written in English. Which one or two should I choose from giant traditions representing hundreds or thousands of published mystics? Look in the *Encyclopedia Britannica* under any religion and its mystical tradition, and you will begin to find major names. The main key for choosing a mystic to study is to find the that one speaks to you personally.

It would also be difficult to recount the major experiences of mystics. This approach doesn't work. It merely presents bits and pieces of trivial differences. I agree with the Hindu formula that we are all climbing the same mountain. It is of little ultimate consequence if my path has scented flowers and yours is all rocks. That we all arrive in the same ultimate unity is really the sole issue.

Therefore, my purpose in this chapter is to throw light on major mystics, all of whom are my kin, so don't take any apparent criticism too seriously, for this is simply an aspect of differences.

Where Mysticism Can Appear in the World

As I've stressed throughout this work, the direct experience of God is a general human potential. I mean this statement without any reservations. This potential occurs across the sexes, age groups, and races. We are in the unfortunate position of knowing little of mystical experience and of being totally remiss in collecting instances. From my experience, I would expect mystical experience to be common in infancy and commonly forgotten, to be dropping in frequency in childhood, largely to disappear in young-adult years when young people are learning to deal with the outer world. But there is surely a resurgence of mystical experience in old age and in the process of dying. The near-death experience is a plain and simple mystical experience, so in dying most are given some enlightenment. Since the experience is everyone's potential, it can occur anywhere. A friend of mine collects incidents of mystical experience that occur in the midst of playing sports. A mystical experience can occur in childbirth. It has occurred to those in prison. I expect it to be fairly common in the mentally handicapped. Why? Because intellectual brilliance is not necessary. Simple openness to experience is. In short, mystical experiences are a human potential for anyone, anywhere, any time.

Despite this, there is a major conditioning by the culture. Some cultures consider the experience of God impossible and invalid; they regard people who have these experiences as psychotic.

In other cultures, including many indigenous groups, the experience will be nearly universal. It has occurred more commonly in the monastic life where quiet reflection on sacred writings is encouraged. Not to have the experience in a full Hindu/Buddhist life would be something of a surprise. Thus, cultural expectations and support of mystical experience play a major role. Another important factor is the extent to which the individual seeks the experience and enters upon regular spiritual practices.

Cultures and given spiritual practices interact. A culture will choose and enforce an approach that has worked for many; so, for example, we have the situation of the American Indian vision quest, in which at adolescence or other special time the seeker goes out on his or her own until a guiding vision is given. I have also seen small groups of ex-drug addicts clearly developing their own ways to discovering Christ as a living force in their lives. This gift was expected, widely talked about, encouraged, and delighted the community when it occurred. So, the overall frequency, intensity, and nature of the experience are in large part in the hands of the culture. Where the experience of God is seen as rare and akin to madness, it will be suppressed and uncommon.

Now some people will suspect that mystical experience is merely a matter of suggestion. What really belies this is the overwhelming tendency for mystics of all cultures and times to drift toward a recognizable universal view. Add to this the fact that this unified and universal view tends to turn up in all religions. And it occurs quite spontaneously in the dying. The culture can see a potential and aid it or suppress it. But with or without the aid of the culture, direct mystical experience can turn up everywhere.

Am I perhaps just being too loose in designating so much as mystical experience? I have found as a mystic that the experience is in a kind of graduated scale. Early experiences often just indicate somehow everything is one and that the person is somehow part of this one. There are stages beyond this, so it is relatively easy to judge the maturity of a mystic. A late state experience occurs when the mystic is shown that only God (or whatever it is called) exists.

One little experience doesn't make a mature mystic, as I stated in chapter one. In later stages, mature mystics do much work to fit their experience into their religious tradition, if they have one. And then, there are mature mystics who were trained by God outside any religion.

We tend to look for simple either/or explanations. What seems to be occurring in world mysticism is an interacting amalgam of several forces:

(1) the intrinsic nature and uniqueness of a person
(2) the mystic's culture
(3) the mystic's religion, if any, and its wisdom literature
(4) God's will in all this.

I see religion as really an aspect of the culture. Like the culture, religion seizes upon aspects it wishes to further and enforces these. One guiding paradigm in this is the culture's handling of male and female roles. There are genuine and consistent biological differences in male and female. The culture takes account of these and enforces what it sees as the best way to handle them. It has some limited scope as to what it can do with these. The universal potential for the experience of God is a given. Culture—and its kin, religion—has a fairly wide scope in what to do with this particular fact. Religions have reacted from the one extreme of actively blocking the experience to the other of intensely fostering it. Yet beyond these is more variability in the system because of the uniqueness of people and the will of God. No one living at the time of Muhammad expected a prophet to arise who would so powerfully and suitably unite the Arab peoples. But it happened.

So, I reiterate that the experience of God is a universal human potential. It may well occur more widely than reported and in unexpected groups such as infants and children simply because we haven't looked for it and are unclear what to look for. Culture and religion play major roles in fostering or suppressing it. Nevertheless, due in part to the uniqueness of each individual and to God's will, the experience of God many appear anywhere and anytime.

Now I will divide the rest of this survey into the major religions, mysticism outside of religions, and the mysticism of Emanuel Swedenborg.

Animism and Indigenous Cultures

Mysticism is so much a human potential that I have reason to expect mature mysticism even in the traditions of indigenous peoples, whom many people mistakenly think of as primitive or undeveloped. Few of these groups have a written language, so their mystical literature is scarce. Many of the better accounts have been done by anthropologists who may give a good written account; but, still, I cannot always trust them to appreciate indigenous mysticism.

A major tendency in indigenous groups is to view everything in their environment as filled with different spirits. They name and interact with all these spirits. Through fasting, or some spiritual trial, they may meet living spirits, even their guardian spirit who may give them their name. I was impressed by Malidoma Somé, an African given extensive Western Catholic training by Jesuits.[1] Somé went back to his people, who considered him a bit far gone for the traditional tribal initiation into their indigenous religion. Their main training is to have the initiate sit before a tree until his particular guardian spirit emerges. What a wonderful way to help adolescents, to help them find their guardian spirit that they can turn to ever after. Somé was slow compared to younger adolescents in the tribe, but finally he met his spirit. He was commissioned by his tribe to represent their ways to others, and he currently lives and lectures in the United States. How does this relate to mysticism? The personal guardian spirit is a representation of the Divine other within. This representation would open up to other more Godlike representations as the person matures.

I do not feel any real difference between aboriginal people and

---

1. Malidoma Somé, *Of Water and the Spirit* (New York: Putnam's, 1994).

myself, except in the multiplicity of their spirits. As a mystic, I am always dealing with the One. But because their general attitude is one of respect for all forms of life, even the animal or plant life they have to kill, I feel sympathy with them. Theirs is basically a life of respect for all that surrounds aborigines That the sun is called one spirit and the stream another would not make any fundamental difference to me. I would expect to learn from their shamans and witch doctors. So, even though I am a well-educated, Western man, I would expect to be able to live comfortably in their world view. I would have to learn the names and ritual for a multiplicity of spirits, but that could be done. There is a general atmosphere of living harmoniously and respectfully with all the spirits that surround us. But why would I not be bothered by the multiplicity? Multiplicity and unity are the same for me. I honor the books that link me to mystics of the past. But I could as easily address them as individuals, as Sir Plotinus or Sir Dionysus. I would feel in harmony with the key element of indigenous religions of striving to live in harmony with all the spirits that surround us. So I would not look down on their ways, but rather would feel honored to be accepted as one of them.

But having become one of them, I would then question the more sensitive of them to determine if they have some sense that these multiple spirits are just aspects of one Great Spirit. I would expect their mystics would say, "Yes." I am sure there have been many great mystics among indigenous peoples. It is sad that they were condemned as pagans and so little evidence of their life experience is left. Because of the openness of indigenous peoples to the spiritual dimension, mysticism is likely to be common among them.

Christianity

Jesus Christ was a mystic in all senses of the term. It appears quite clear that he saw himself as giving meaning to the expected Messiah in Judaism. Like most mystics working in a tradition, he clarified and gave greater meaning to Judaism. But he gave it so much meaning it split off as Christianity. It is also quite common that a great mystic in a faith is viewed as external. That is, the followers have the idea, "He did it, but he was exceptional. I could not hope to go that way." This also happened in the followers of the mystic Swedenborg. So every word of the Great One is studied and gone over, and a massive literature of commentaries develops.

Yet there is an underlying theme in Christ's own ministry. The Apostles were trained to be like him and to go out and teach. The letters of Paul in the New Testament clearly spell out the way of imitating Christ until the individual finds the Christ within. And, indeed, early Christian communities seemed to consist in being loving like Jesus.

The Christian Church used to be one church. About the year 1000, the church split between the Roman Catholics in the West and the Eastern Orthodox Church in the East. It is important to understand these two churches because they represent an almost opposite understanding of mystics and of how to handle them. In many ways the Eastern Orthodox Church, even though Christian, is closer to the Eastern religions. The Orthodox Church is partly divided by ethnicities into Russian, Greek, Coptic (Egyptian), Bulgarian, etc. Yet these scattered groups are in communion. The Orthodox Church resembles Christianity in the early centuries. The early mystical literature is seen as important and widely studied. Church members seek deification (that a person can join in the life of God). The Church declares itself mystical. It has fostered a great many mystics, particularly in the monastic life. A life given to reflection on sacred literature, meditation, and prayer easily fosters the experience of God. One of their great mystics is St. Seraphim of Sarov (1754–1833) who healed countless people, so many no one counted or kept track of them. He healed even the blind and lame. His brother monks were somewhat annoyed because so many people lined up to see him.

Orthodox mystics have always been recognized and treasured. Many were asked to become bishops. With less monastic life in general, mysticism has partially faded as more people became involved in external things. But in its extensive use of icons (which, as the previous chapter shows, are windows into the spiritual) and honoring its ancient literature and mystics, mysticism lies just below the surface in the Eastern Orthodox Church.

The Roman Catholic Church took almost an opposite course. In the Orthodox Church, a man had to be a monk to become a bishop or religious leader. That is, he had to be deeply imbued with the religious life. The Roman Church, on the other hand, took European monarchy as its model. The Pope is a monarch. As a political form, the church became autocratic. The Orthodox Church is more democratic. At the height of the monastic movement, the Catholic Church developed many significant mystics, but they became something of a threat. Here were people who claim to have contacted God without going through priest and pope! The Roman Church has a remarkable history of mistreating mystics. The great Meister Eckhart was excommunicated. Others were killed, tried for heresy, exiled, not allowed to speak or write, etc. You might think that today the Church knows better; but in recent years, the Roman Catholic mystic Teillard de Chardin was forbidden to publish. Even today there are mystics under censure. This tells us a couple of things. There are church authorities, supposedly steeped in the wisdom of God, unable to recognize or accept the direct experience of God. Another is that mysticism tends to flower under monasticism even when not really welcomed.

And what of Protestant sects? There are so many splits in this group one almost needs a weekly bulletin on the new churches. It is as though the direct experience of God is not known in the Protestant churches, not sought, and not encouraged. So it is officially absent. Excluding Emanuel Swedenborg, who was raised as a Lutheran, I would be hard put to come up with two real mystics in this group. Even some reported to be mystics seem very light, borderline, and questionable.

But it is necessary to make a major proviso. It is at the official church level that mystics are rare in the Western Christian churches. The direct experience of God is not recognized or sought after. But a careful study of any church group could turn up thousands of mystics. These are people who have integrated their religion and have been in personal communication with God a long time. Often such mystics end up in some service to others as a way to express their understanding of God. There are many Christians living in harmony with others and being of service who are mystics whether or not their church cares. I would expect to find mature mystics especially in the aged, even though many of them are unsure what mysticism means.

The Christian church stems from one of the world's great mystics. The Eastern Orthodox branch has retained much of the earliest form and values of the early Christian church. It is openly mystical and honors great mystics as saints. The Roman Catholic and Protestant churches either don't encourage mysticism or have difficulty with it when it appears.

Judaism

Judaism is, of course, the very root of Christianity. Most of the Christian Bible is the Hebrew Bible (the Old Testament). Early Jewish mysticism existed in the prophets, who experienced major visions that were brought back to the people as a criticism of their morality. This is a particular aspect of Judaism since most mystics find their own way, not the way of a people. Another unusual feature is that Judaism is an ethnic religion. One can convert into it, but it is largely seen as an integral part of the Jewish people. A friend of mine converted to Judaism and reports it was like being given a whole new family with extended relatives. Also it is an unusual religion that exists in a covenant with God. Add to this extensive persecution down through history, and the stage is set for differences.

The Jewish culture itself trains in religion by a good deal of reading of sacred texts, discussion, and argument. The Kabbalah is widely regarded as Jewish mysticism. But a study of it shows this is not what world mysticism is all about. And many Jewish scholars agree that "the Kabbalah is by definition an esoteric body of speculation."[2]

As I have been at some pains to point out, world mysticism is neither esoteric nor speculative. Real mystics discover God. Personal speculation is really inappropriate in this situation. The Kabbalah is esoteric, seen as penetrable only by the few. Even the Jewish spiritual practices Idel describes are unusually stressful and unlike those practiced in the rest of the world. There is some difficulty in directly experiencing God in all the Western religions, but this seems particularly marked in the Jewish realm. I was so taken aback by the lack of mysticism in the Kabbalah I had to consult other experts on this.

Avran Davis says the Jews lost their major religious leaders in the Holocaust.[3] But beyond this, there are other signs of difficulty. It is a Jewish canon of teaching in this area that the mystical union is not possible. The person always retains his or her personal identity. This suggests few religious leaders ever experienced the mystical union, which, as we have seen, is common in other religions. In an intense mystical experience, the little ego/self disappears in the life of God. The ego returns later as the experience wears off, but a loss of self-identity is a common trait of mystical union. Briefly said then, Judaism seems to have little true mystical experience.

But realize now we are speaking of the official religion. A religion can overlook or suppress mysticism, but it arises anyway. The Hasidic movement among poor Jews in eastern Europe is a fine example of Jewish mysticism. The official church authorities reacted against it, much as the Roman Catholic hierarchy reacted to their own mystics. Hasidism translated Jewish teachings into a colorful mysticism. It is a mysticism of human fellowship and

---

2. Moshe Idel, *Kabbalah* (New Haven, Conn.: Yale University Press, 1988), 255.

3. Avram Davis, *The Way of the Flame* (San Francisco: Harper, 1996), 16. Davis found mysticism in Buddhism and now instructs Jews in Buddhist ways adapted to the Jewish tradition.

love, often with an ecstatic character. One of its main tools is human stories that illustrate its mysticism.[4]

The use of stories to convey mysticism is also common in Zen, in indigenous groups, and in Christian parables, among others. Beyond the Hasidim, there are unrecognized mystics in the midst of Judaism. A most impressive one is the contemporary Jewish seminary professor Abraham Joshua Heschel. Although he does not profess to be a mystic, Heschel is a most gifted one. He is an excellent example of a real mystic giving greater depth of meaning to his own tradition. So Judaism as an official religion seems partly mistaken about mysticism, but it has arisen anyway. There are many Jews carefully following their ways and welcomed in heaven.

Islam

I early on found and enjoyed the Islamic mystics, the Sufis. But I must profess that the Koran and Islam in general seem far away to me. I have found the Koran repetitive and badly organized, although I am willing to admit that this may indicate simply that I have not been educated in the Koran. I love Islamic architecture and design. Arabic script, used in quotations of the Koran, I find quite beautiful, even though I cannot read it. I also appreciate the link between science and religion in Islam.[5] But Islam itself seemed a bit distant and alien until I read the Sufis.

More and more translations of Sufis are becoming available, particularly of the ecstatic poet Rumi. I also quite enjoy Kabir and the contemporary Pir Vilayat Khan.[6] When reading the Sufi

---

4. Martin Buber, *Tales of the Hasidim* (New York: Schocken, 1991).

5. A good work on this particular topic is Seyyed Nasr, *Science and Civilization in Islam* (New York: Barnes and Noble, 1968).

6. Pir Vilayat Khan, *Samadhi with Open Eyes* (New Lebanon, New York: Sufi Order, 1978) and *Introducing Spirituality into Counseling and Therapy* (New Lebanon, New York: Omega, 1982). Jalal Al-Din Rumi, *The Essential Rumi*, trans. Coleman Barks (San Francisco: Harper San Francisco: 1997). *The Kabir Book: Forty-Four of the Ecstatic Poems of Kabir*, ed. Robert Bly (Boston: Beacon Press, 1977; rpt. 1993).

writings, I have not the slightest doubt that these people are describing the direct experience of God. But what surprises me is that this experience is somehow constrained into a particular form by the culture of Islam. Sufis are practically the masters of the ecstatic, loving, feelingful description of the experience of God. They do this well, but the experience of God in their hands lacks other dimensions. Perhaps the other dimensions are somewhere else in the Sufi literature.

The famous Rubaiyat of Omar Kayyam is an example of Sufi mysticism. To many, it is often seen as simply praise of life's pleasures. But when seen as a thinly disguised love relationship to Allah, it takes on a deeper meaning. Being drunk on wine is to be caught up in the spiritual. Omar hated falsity and the religious pretensions of his time, so he expressed his mystical experience in this form. The book resembles the Bible's Song of Solomon, which can also be seen as a love affair or something a good deal more. The Rubaiyat influenced other Sufis to express their experiences in this form.

Hinduism

When I am in Islam, I am in the land of one book, the Koran, and limited and consistent religious practices that are fairly true of the entire Islamic world. However, as I step into Hinduism, I find myself in another world. For one, Hinduism is extremely ancient, making Islam and Christianity fairly recent innovations. In marked contrast to Christianity, which fractures over every difference, Hinduism is extremely tolerant of differences. A Hindu might ask another Hindu, "Which God do you pray to?" And Hinduism has a vast number of Gods known to be aspects of the One God. Each village, home, or person can create or find their own God. I would despair of understanding all the Gods, all their signs, and all the rituals.

But Hinduism is vast in quite another sense. Hinduism began

before the fairly recent division of human knowledge into various fields and so became involved with all aspects of life as a unity. Healing, for instance—what we now call medicine—was a part of the religion itself. Many of the separate fields we now know—geology, mathematics, cosmology, etc.—were all started in Hinduism. Moreover, the Hindus seem to be particularly searching and ready for inward discovery. A major part of Hindu exploration has been, from the beginning, the search for the living God. The search for God is an open, respected, and avowed goal. Because Hinduism tolerates differences, it has collected the results of a remarkable number of spiritual experiments.

As an outsider coming upon Hinduism, I am almost overwhelmed by their religious richness and their long history of mysticism. The Upanishads comes out of an ancient oral tradition and was finally set in writing about 300 BCE. These writings represent some of the purest and most far-searching mysticism in existence. In spite of its being ancient and Hindu, when I read the Upanishads, it is quite like coming home to a familiar place. The central idea is that ultimately only God exists. This is precisely what I found centuries later. The vast richness of Hinduism is a little intimidating. I do not know that I could ever master it. But Hindu mysticism is as clear and rich and full of discovery as any mysticism on earth. It would be difficult to cite even their principal mystics, for there have been so many. Probably a large proportion of Hindus are genuine mystics! How many Western religions could say this? The yogas are just a division of the forms of approach to God. Each yoga has a vast literature of many methods actually practiced by mystics in the past and still today. Although there is speculation, and even occultism, among Hindus, their mystics are all seasoned practitioners of a spiritual way. Whereas the Sufis seem to me to be constrained into one form, Hindu mysticism has quite probably explored every nook and cranny of mysticism. It is almost its richness and overabundance that are the main difficulty of Hindu mysticism.

Buddhism

It became apparent to me when I wrote of Hinduism that I was also showing the reason that Buddhism arose. Over the centuries Hinduism has gone through periods of losing its way and finding it. It appears that, in the time of Siddhartha Gautama, the Buddha, Hinduism was bogged down in speculation and spiritual practices that were not working. Buddha tried the Hindu ways of his time and failed. He appeared to have an abiding need, not just to find his way to the All, but also to undo the root of human suffering. I have no doubt he found the All and is one of the greatest mystics. Buddhism is a very clear path. Initially the path leads into simple rules as to how to live to lessen human sorrow (The Triple Gems and The Eight Fold Path). But this same path also lays a foundation that leads to the experience of the All. So, whereas Hinduism is almost overabundantly rich in having explored everything, Buddhism is almost solely attempting to lead people to mysticism. I can no longer say "God" in Buddhism because our Western personified, anthropomorphic God is not what the Buddhists ultimately found.

Out of the muddy richness and complexity of Hinduism arose the Buddhist lotus. Buddhism functions well all the way down to the lowest social level with simple rules that lessen sorrow and increase meaningful living and are an excellent beginning to approach the experience of God. But beyond this level, Buddhism has accumulated over the centuries a vast treasure house of mystics and their findings on spiritual practices. I believe one could fairly say Buddhism is the polishing and perfecting of the mystical aspects of Hinduism.

I have one criticism of Buddhism. Buddhism has had a major portion of the world's mystics, yet if you search for descriptions of their experiences of the Ultimate, there is relatively little direct experience of God. Buddha warned against telling others of your spiritual experience. The reason is clear. It can lead to vanity and losing the treasure of the Way. Buddhists have mostly followed this injunction. There is certainly a real danger in a youth's saying, "I have met the Buddha nature, so I am superior." This is a genuine danger in youth but far less so in older, mature mystics. As I have said repeatedly, I see great use in mystics' describing their experience to help others to know what it is like. You can safely reveal things if your real intent is to aid others, rather than to elevate yourself. Considering that probably most of the world's mature mystics can be found in the Buddhist tradition, there are far too few descriptions of the experience coming out of Buddhism.

Thus, I would soften Buddha's injunction. Beginners on the way should keep silent on their experiences, except to tell other mystics. But when they get gray hairs and maturity, all clarifications on the Way for others will be welcome, even though there are limits to how well all this can be put in words. Words are never the way. They are only pointers, and understanding their very meaning depends on being on the Way.

As probably the second oldest religion on earth (Hinduism may be the first), Buddhism is a giant edifice with different schools and forms of mysticism. I feel at home in Zen. I love it when the experience of God is captured in a haiku poem, a flower arrangement, a garden, or a Zen story. In the artistic side of Zen, the great search has come home in simple beauty. I consider the whole Buddhist spiritual experience, texts, and art one of the great treasures of humankind. The current systematic destruction of the people and culture of Tibet by the Chinese Communists is one of the crimes of the century. Tibetan Buddhism is a graduate school of mysticism.

Mystics outside of Religious Traditions

Mysticism has been so closely associated with established religion that it might lead one to believe religion is the only way to the experience of God. Yet, in organized religion, genuine mystics tend to arise *in spite of* the religion, so I have likened mysticism to wildflowers that manage to grow anywhere. That is, it appears here and there in individuals almost in disregard of their prevailing culture. The experience of God is so much a human potential that we can expect it to arise in individuals who are not formal members of any church. It is this group I now look at.

One of the central difficulties is that we are really speaking of those who have known the experience of God *who publish,* and their publication becomes available in the mainstream. We must bear this in mind, for behind writer mystics are countless unknown mystics who do not publish and do not become known. If we had to search out these people, we would best look among those who are extraordinarily well regarded for the good they did to society. Why in those who do good works? Simply because a close relationship to God often results in some sort of giving back to society of the joyous grace mystics have received. They may not be writers, nor may they be anything like theologians with a well-formulated doctrine. This spirit of giving back was in the medieval cathedral builders. I have clearly seen it in some who care for animals. A lovely way of giving back is in gardening. In fact, there is no limit in the variety of ways in which it can be expressed. There is some sort of work we love to do. It is also what we are best at. So unknown mystics end up giving back to the world along the lines of what they enjoy, what they almost have to do. Abandon all thought that their way has to look "religious." It can be in any area of human endeavor.

You then have to look internally at what their contribution means to them. Mahatma Gandhi looked to some like a politician. But if you looked internally at his ends, it was never Gandhi—the man himself and his own selfish ends—he was working for. It was justice itself, regardless of what sacrifices it called on him to perform. The difference is subtle. If you look at the work of many politicians, they are working for their reputation, their standing, etc.; the good they do is incidental to their own self-aggrandizement. Gandhi worked at transcendent justice; it was woven in his every act. He neglected Gandhi the man.

The mystic as a craftsman does a good job at a fair price and is aware of his or her craft as a contribution to mankind. To a mystic this is part of the ongoing relationship to God; they give because they enjoy it. Many people think the mystic must do something earth-shaking. This is untrue. The mystic's internal spiritual end is to aid creation. When I wrote on Swedenborg's philosophy of uses as a spiritual way, many were surprised at how small the uses were of which I spoke.[7] The mystic's end is to aid creation in even the smallest acts. Two persons clean up a place. One may be communing with God, while the other is just sweeping. Outwardly there may be little difference; but inwardly, spiritually, the difference is great. If you worked with both of them, you would soon feel the difference.

In some ways, it is easier to become a mystic outside of organized religion. In organized religion, you feel constrained by certain ways and certain texts. Outside, you feel freer to explore all possibilities. Your favorite literature can come from any culture, any time, and any subject. We are in an age more blessed with the riches of the past than any prior age. The great Swedenborg had none of the Hindu–Buddhist literature, yet I can now get all that I want. It is as though each age has its blessings and drawbacks. The mystic outside of churches now has to sort through an incredible wealth of literature. But rather than never having known Plotinus or Pseudo-Dionysius, I would rather have the task of sorting through piles of such works.

I certainly see an advantage to age and maturity for a mystic on his or her own. So much that children and adolescents suffer over in old age seems as nothing. In age you can look back at a greater breadth of experience. In age your life's values have been hammered out and tested. "Life" is no longer a high-flown concept. I recently saw a lovely Russian painting of an old Mongol peasant. All the wrinkles and creases were clearly painted. He would know what I am talking about.

On the other hand, there is also a disadvantage to mystics

---

7. "Uses: A Way of Personal and Spiritual Growth," *The Country of Spirit: Selected Writings* (San Francisco: J. Appleseed & Co., 1992), 61–87.

outside of churches. In churches, central doctrines are presented over and over again. In the churches that genuinely foster mysticism, such as the Eastern Orthodox, there are spiritual practices you can use to keep on the way. Outside of churches, there is greater freedom, but also more distraction. It is no accident so many mystics arose out of the monastic life. Outside of churches, too often people die without even having taken time to sum up what it is all about, before they venture into the greater spiritual world. So, while mysticism is possible outside organized religion, the lack of a religious guide, coupled with a wider, freer world, has its drawbacks.

Lastly, let me just broach a problem I have long thought about. I suspect there is a very wide, even gigantic realm of hidden or quasi-mystics. It is clear in the arts. These are people who worship a god named Beauty. If you look at their spiritual internals, they look like mystics in all respects except there is no conventional God. Similarly, there are people for whom love, human justice, the beauty of nature, the care of children, etc., are paramount. They admire, enjoy, and participate in some elevated aspect of creation. In their internal spiritual function, they closely resemble mystics except they do not acknowledge God. Now which is more central to mysticism: acknowledging God or a way of living? There are scoundrels bound for hell who acknowledge God. I believe it is a way of living that is central. These hidden mystics honor some aspect of existence as more important than themselves. Instead of a formal declaration of "Yes, you exist, my God," they have a harmonious way of being in creation while aiding the general human enterprise. These people are clearly outside churches since the term and concept of "God" is often uncomfortable for them. These hidden mystics honor God in whatever aspect of creation they honor. It is actually a small step from honoring a lovely stream to the One Spirit, a mere shift of scale. The internal workings and the spirit are the same.

I said this group is gigantic. Among others, it includes the countless parents—especially mothers—to whom care for children is a sacred enterprise. This group of hidden mystics would include a large proportion of humanity. Whenever a person honors and respects something other than him- or herself, that person approaches the All.

Emanuel Swedenborg

For a long while I thought of Emanuel (meaning: God is with us) Swedenborg as simply a Western mystic. It was not until I had explored the world's mystics that it began to dawn on me that Swedenborg was literally a giant among the world's mystics. How is he a giant? In 1745, God granted him permission to explore all the spiritual worlds beyond this one. Swedenborg did so; and, as was his habit, he carefully set down all he found in an extraordinary exploration of heaven and hell for the last twenty-seven years of his life. Of course, all mystics explore the spiritual, but to have such a lengthy and detailed exploration of heaven and hell appears to be unique in human history.

Swedenborg's findings are detailed in his work *Heaven and Hell*.[8] As I explored the world's mystics, I fully expected some others would report on the worlds beyond this one. There are important hints in the Tibetan Book of the Dead; but I soon found that various mystical traditions, particularly the Christian, compiled a patchwork of guesses based on their sacred texts. None of these begins to compare to the clarity and coherence of Swedenborg's *Heaven and Hell*. It began to dawn on me that the man I had known of for some years, and had even written on,[9] was truly unusual.

To begin with, Swedenborg was a very systematic scientist, quite accustomed to learning new fields and summarizing what he

---

8. Emanuel Swedenborg, *Heaven and Its Wonders and Hell, from Things Seen and Heard*, trans. John C. Ager, second edition (West Chester, Penna.: Swedenborg Foundation, 1995); and *Heaven and Hell*, trans. George F. Dole (West Chester, Penna.: Swedenborg Foundation, 1976).

9. Wilson Van Dusen, *The Presence of Other Worlds* (West Chester, Penna.: Chrysalis Books, 1991).

found. He felt his life in science was really just a preparation for his later work as a revelator. And I agree. Who best to enter and explore the worlds beyond this one than a man whose whole life was a preparation for this work? He is unique in the sheer breadth and depth of his spiritual experiences. I remarked earlier how central humility is in mystics. Most of his great heavenly revelations were presented anonymously as a "servant of the Lord, Jesus Christ." Only late in life did he feel permitted to put his own name on his religious works. Here is another sign of his humility. Though he appeared to record everything, he never mentioned certain miraculous powers he had, not even in his private notes. All of the nearly miraculous powers he showed were reported by people around him. But let me, for a moment, look at the background of this giant.[10]

Emanuel Swedenborg (1688–1772) was born the son of prominent Lutheran bishop in Sweden. Later the family was ennobled, and Baron Swedenborg served in the Swedish House of Lords. He became known for trying to prevent war and for learned presentations on the economy. Though his father wanted Emanuel to serve in the church, the young man was fascinated with all things of science. He made his living as one of the leading mining engineers of Sweden; as such, he traveled, observed, and brought back new designs for mining equipment. He mastered all of the scientific knowledge of his time. He first formulated the nebular hypothesis, preceding Kant and Laplace in this theory. He wrote a number of volumes on anatomy. He spoke twelve languages. He invented a number of things including a flying machine. In many areas, he was in advance of most of contemporary scientists, for example, in the study of brain anatomy.

How did Swedenborg turn from a scholar, who had to know

---

10. There are numerous biographies of Swedenborg available, including George Trobridge, *Swedenborg: Life and Teaching,* rev. R. H. Tafel and R. H. Tafel, Jr. (New York: Swedenborg Foundation, 1992); Signe Toksvig, *Emanuel Swedenborg: Scientist and Mystic* (New York: Swedenborg Foundation, 1983); and George F. Dole and Robert H. Kirven, *A Scientist Explores Spirit* (West Chester, Penna.: Chrysalis Books, 1997).

everything, into being a mystic and revelator? Having mastered most fields of science, he went on a search for the soul. In this inward search, he tried a number of methods. Bear in mind that none of the Hindu–Buddhist literature on spiritual practices was available to him. His search took him through a careful study of inner states and of his own dreams. His *Journal of Dreams* may be the longest, oldest, and best-interpreted dream diary in existence.[11] He was not only working on dreams, however; he also discovered the hypnagogic state and trance in this period. His private notes give the distinct impression of a sincere seeker after God. After two years of spiritual crisis, he experienced a vision of Jesus, who gave him access to the spiritual world. He made copious notes on spiritual experiences and learned Hebrew so he could read the Hebrew Bible in its original form. He already knew Greek for the New Testament. After this preparation and four years of exploration of the spiritual realm, he began issuing the *Arcana Coelestia* (Heavenly Secrets).[12] The change in writing from that of a scientist to a mystic was quite marked. His scientific writing was restrained and rational, whereas his spiritual writing seems to be by an inspired new man. Even two-and-a-half centuries later, I feel we do not fully understand all the implications of the *Arcana*. Swedenborg felt his main task in this work was to open up the interior sense of the Bible. According to him, the Bible has two levels of meaning, the literal meaning that most understand and a deeper, richer, far more human and spiritual inner sense. He gives so many thousands of examples of this it becomes quite convincing. I regard the whole matter of the internal sense in its full use and implications as beyond my own understanding. In addition to revealing this internal sense of the Bible, he started to describe the whole nature and design of creation.

---

11. J. J. G. Wilkinson, trans. *Swedenborg's Journal of Dreams, 1743–1744.* With commentary by Wilson Van Dusen (New York: Swedenborg Foundation, 1986).

12. Emanuel Swedenborg, *Arcana Coelestia,* trans. John F. Potts, 12 volumes (West Chester, Penna.: Swedenborg Foundation, 1995–1998).

Why is Swedenborg not better known? I have seen major surveys of mystics that do not even mention him. His works have been translated and kept available since his death. Without his work in mysticism, he could easily be known now as a great early scientist of the stature of Leonardo Da Vinci. I and others feel the sheer size and extraordinary nature of his spiritual findings overshadowed his work as a scientist. He is too big to pigeonhole easily and understand.

There are several premises one should bear in mind in looking at his spiritual works:.

(1) Although he was a giant intellect, Swedenborg presents his findings as simply and directly as possible. He wrote in Latin, the universal language of scholars in his day, but in a simple, straight-forward Latin.

(2) In no case is he allowed by God to speculate or to borrow from anyone else. He is always reporting actual experiences.

(3) Swedenborg describes the Universal, but in Christian terms. It is fairly common for mystics to report their understanding of the Universal in the terms of their own religion.

(4) Swedenborg's most central finding—that ultimately only the Lord exists—is also the central finding of the Hindu Upanishads, which he never saw.

I regard Swedenborg as weak on spiritual practices compared to Hinduism and Buddhism. But it was quite enough of a task in his time to try to show the world the universal design of creation. His description of the life after this one is quite beyond any other in existence I have seen.

In a real sense, his spiritual findings are both utterly simple and very complex. If I may, let me evoke a Tibetan spiritual joke to illustrate this. A yak's tail is both simple (it's just a yak's tail) or complex if you start examining the hair, skin, bones, and the nerves within and the life that animates it. So, when a student or scholar begins to get too involved, the master says, "Oh, don't forget that it is really just a yak's tail!" What is the yak's tail of Swedenborg's findings? The nature of the human is an image of the design of creation. Simple and profound. Thus, Swedenborg is a unique and largely unknown giant among the world's mystics.

A Map of World Religions

While reflecting on the matters just dealt with, it gradually came to me that world religions and mysticism fall into a pattern. This will be sketched here in broad strokes. Don't expect precision. We are now looking at the entire world.

First, there is a principal to understand. The experience of God is a universal human potential. Whatever the form of a religion, no matter how strange its imagery and doctrines, mystical experience arises when the individual comes into a personal relationship with the Ultimate, whatever it is called. For instance, the Native American on a vision quest is working on mysticism; it is more likely that the missionary out to convert him is far from the direct experience.

I envision a map of the world's religions, which is partly geographic and partly functional because we are dealing with how religions work. Imagine a north and south longitudinal line that goes through the Holy Land at about 35 degrees east longitude. This divides the world into western and eastern halves. Because it is so apt, we take the main symbol of Byzantium as a symbol of all this—an eagle with spread wings and two heads, one facing west and the other east. This is now part of the armorial symbols of many countries. Constantinople (now Istanbul) was the capital of the Byzantine empire and literally was on the boundary of east and west. In symbolic terms, to go east is to head toward the inner and direct spiritual experience. To go west is to travel toward the outer world of things.

Roughly on the line through the Holy Land, three great religions were born: Judaism, Christianity, and Islam (put in their historical order). Islam and Judaism even today have and Christianity in the past had a similar ethos. These religions were marked by a strong sense that we are fortunate to have been given a way to love one another and to approach God. They had a strong sense of being an enlightened people who express this in loving their own people. This was their mysticism of love and fellowship. In Islam, believers literally come together in Mecca. Early Christianity was a loving sharing community. When Judaism came into a mystical flowering in later centuries in Hasidism, it was very much this sort of community. All three were peoples of the Book. Let us consider that love and fellowship are almost a root experience that dawns around this line.

Time marches on and all three groups scatter to the west. Islam and Eastern Orthodox Christianity also went east, but we will deal with that later. It is quite as though the religions that went west underwent a fairly consistent cultural change. They became more external. They fought over doctrinal differences. They also became more rational. The one original Christian church split, with western Roman Catholics leaving the democratic organization of the early church and setting up essentially a monarchy with a pope at the head. Judaism turned to endless discussion and study of its Word. The Arab people made major contributions to the foundation of western technology. They gave us our number system and much else. As the externalized religions that these three became, the experience of God is almost unknown except among rare individuals. All three western branches at times did not appreciate the rise of any mysticism and engaged in various kinds of suppression. That is what external religions do: they suppress disruptive people who claim to know God because they are a threat to church order and church authority.

But meanwhile, the external, rational bent of externalized religions prepares the way for science and technology. It almost appears that a whole society can develop the inner or the outer, but not likely both. The western advance of religions across Europe and to the North American continent developed the outer marvels of science and technology.

Now let us head east of this line. Christianity exists as the Eastern Orthodox Church, an avowedly mystical church. Islam went both west and east. In its eastern component, Sufism arose, Islam's own mysticism. The general march east is into personal exploration. We find the immense and varied inward exploration of Hinduism and yoga. Then we have Buddhism going all the way to the Pacific Ocean. Buddha himself was a Hindu who founded Buddhism as a clarification of the ways to the experience of God. The entire eastward way was poor in science and technology, but was rich in inward exploration and in exploring ways to the experience of God.

Even in some detail, this layout of religions is fairly accurate. The Eastern Orthodox Church only went part-way east and is poorer on spiritual practices than Buddhism, which went further east. Swedenborg from Sweden (about longitude 20 degrees east) was a scientist (characteristic west of the line) who, even though a mystic, brought order to religion (a western tendency). As a natural mystic, I have found Zen Buddhism easiest to understand and picked up other forms of Buddhism, Hinduism, the Eastern Orthodox, and Sufism in that order—a trip from the extreme east to the west.

The symbol chosen for all this is the double-headed eagle that looks both east and west. If you consider it, east and west are two halves of a whole called Earth, our home. Could it be difficult for people to develop both the inner and the outer way at the same time? It seems so. As a natural mystic, I was set back by the western general obtuseness about mystical experience. Perhaps this division was the best way to develop these contrary eastern and western values.

As a result, we mystics can have our abundance of books from various times and cultures. Remember, when all this started, books were copied by hand. To own one book was quite rare. It is technology that provides inexpensive books. We are now in a wonderful interchange of knowledge with the worldwide Internet. So, I am a modern mystic with over 2,000 books, with the *Encyclopedia Britannica* on two compact disks, and practically instant communication to anywhere in the world, thanks to technology. The older mystics never had it so good.

There is another worldwide historical dimension to all this. In spite of varied time, cultures, and circumstances, religions have been in fairly consistent development. The earliest religions deal with the forces of nature as aspects of the Divine. These forces are approached with prayer, sacrifice, and ceremony. Or various aspects of the nature around these early worshipers are named spirits; the spirit of a tree, rock, or stream are prayed to or appeased. At this early stage, God is divided into various spirits and natural forces. A later stage occurs when all these externals are gathered into one sacred animal (the bull of Assyria, the Mayan feathered serpent, etc.). The Divine is still out there but at least in a single creature that is other than human. The next stage arises when God is recognized in an emissary (Muhammad in Islam, Moses in Judaism). God then has emissaries and intermediaries that people can relate to. Also God begins to seem human or human-like. A later stage occurs when God is seen as incarnate in a person (Jesus Christ, a Hindu avatar). Often, in addition to this, there is either a teaching or an intuition that there is a One beyond manifestation (Allah in Islam, Brahman in the Hindu, the Father in Christianity). Thus, religions begin scattered in many nonhuman forms, become focused in an animal and later in human figures and representations. There is a slow conversion to a human form with the strong implication that God is like us and may even be approached through our own inner life. Mystical religions that treasure spiritual practices and lead to the experience of God simply carry this to the next step. They teach ways into the direct personal experience of God, enabling persons to find the Way for themselves. Ancient religions sacrificed everything but themselves. Later religions sacrifice one's self. So, over time, God becomes like us, and then within and highly accessible. Religions gradually gather into the innermost life of the individual.

I hope by now the question of which is the best religion seems a little foolish. First, we would have to ask the question of best for whom. Then, we would have to understand the person and the culture. It comes down to whatever leads to good conduct; respect for others and for creation itself is quite acceptable. The different religions and their individual explorations enrich the whole.

Chapter Ten

The Cosmic Order

I T OFTEN SEEMS AS IF OUR EX-
istence is too rich and varied. When images flash by on a television
screen it is a fitting representation of our lives. There are too many
possibilities. We are inundated with ads, with miracle cures and
invitations to try this and that. Then people come and interrupt
us. The doorbell and telephone ring. It is like a merry-go-round,
delightful at times, but also repetitive. This is the engrossing
round of events, the Hindu-Buddhist *samsara*. Even if our focus
were limited to religion, there is the same *samsara*. Which religion?
Many religions would send their ads and spokesmen to come to
the door. There are so many apparently competing doctrines.
Which way to go? If we were on a real merry-go-round, we would
like to go to the controls in the center and shut it off. Then, in the
silence, we can gaze at the surrounding park, and each other, and
slowly make sense of it all.

This is essentially what meditation or other spiritual practices do. They shut off the whirl of events so we can come to experience our own center, which also happens to be the center of the universe. At the center, we come into peace; and, slowly, in our subtle understanding, we get a sense of the order of existence. At the center, we can explore the central nature of things. An early discovery is that it is a free and peaceful place. Even though in meditation all deliberate effort is suspended, it is also an early discovery that the background of mental processes go on anyway. Feelings come and go. Whole complex ideas are suddenly known. It begins to become apparent that there are currents of life in us which we know little about. This creates a certain natural humility and modesty about how central and in control we are. Creative people learn to recognize and give expression to these processes. This is how we accomplish more than we thought possible. For example, when I quit serious writing to eat, I am accustomed to some editor in me suggesting specific changes, which I dutifully note down while biting into a sandwich.

Mystical experience is simply a spontaneous and unexpected deepening during a visit to one's center. The Universal shows itself. You feel a joyous and elevated state. Love opens up and shows its wonder. You may simply realize intense feeling and sense Presence. If you have long sought an answer to something, it may be given now. It is natural to honor such experiences privately and to seek to return to them. Over time you learn ways to this experience so it becomes more accessible. Among some mystics, this joy can be experienced nearly all the time.

Since mystical experience has been so much emphasized, it is a fair question to ask what good are habitual visits to one's center and the sometimes collateral mystical experiences. There are so many benefits involved. Basically, mysticism is a process of coming to open up and to become aware of the wellsprings of your own life and, incidentally, of all life. Out of this arises self-understanding and humility. The process naturally corrects your faults, which are impediments to going further. Both physical and mental healing is possible this way. It affects your values. It also can lead to your own love of life, which in Swedenborg's terms is your nature and your highest joy and use in the world. In effect, visits to your center tend to correct everything that is wrong.

I can amplify this by looking at the effects of the repeated experiences of God. In some deep and unfathomable way, they put in order your whole relationship to this existence and to your eternity. They may deepen whatever religious faith you have, or they can lead into the universal of religion. For instance, mystical experiences can make a Muslim a better Muslim, but because of the contact with the Universal, it may also make a Muslim more tolerant of other religions. I could go on at great length expanding on the implications of these benefits.

All this is the potential of every person. Moreover, it is fairly easy to come by.[1] The ways to these direct experiences are known in some cultures and widely practiced, while almost unknown in others. It would be relatively easy to classify religions by how well they foster the experience of God because some emphasize that the student should take up a spiritual practice, while others hardly know what spiritual practice is. Religions that emphasize direct personal experience treasure approaches they have seen work over the centuries. Religions that foster mystical experience de-emphasize doctrine because understanding and doctrine should arise out of personal experience rather than academic study. Such religions also have people who are master teachers of a Way. It is the difference between thought about the truth and the personal discovery of it. The way of personal discovery subtly reforms the person; thought does not. It is the difference between reading about bicycle-riding and the gyroscopic effect of wheels, etc., and actually riding a bicycle about town.

So, in mystical experience we have what is absolutely central to human existence. Yet it is little known and little fostered. On the

---

1. I explain this in some detail in my work *Returning to the Source* (Moab, Utah: Real People Press, 1996).

surface the various religions appear like competing enterprises trying to gather members. Yet seen spiritually they all in their own way drift toward the Divine Center.

The Roman Catholic Church emphasizes the Mass,
yet the way to the Holy Center is there.
The Salvation Army emphasizes helping others,
yet the way is surely there too.
Primitives may emphasize a way through ancestors,
but these ancestors have become spiritual beings,
And there is surely a way there too.
Eastern Orthodox silently recite the Jesus Prayer,
and Hindus and Buddhists a mantra,
and there is surely a way too.
The Jews have a way through the sacred history of their people,
and there is a way too.

Can you conceive a God so broad as to deal easily, internally, and simultaneously with all these ways? Should you despair at cultural differences? Is it not a wonder that there are so many ways? The Hindu image is that we are all climbing a great mountain toward the supreme goal. We are on different paths up this mountain. Ultimately, it doesn't matter which way you take because they all reach the top. And every path leads forward from right here, wherever you are now. You are already on your path and have been for a long while.

This image of all climbing a mountain by different paths is a fitting image of the whole mystical enterprise. We naturally think of a religion as a single path up the mountain, but because of the extent of individual differences, we are each on a different path. The mountain is that great. There is a dilemma in presenting mysticism. On the one hand, it is utterly simple and immediate. How can anyone make a book out of that? Yet, we are in the midst of immense differences, the differences of individuals and of religions. I have the abiding sense of the mystical as simple and immediate, but every time it is described it is as though I journey through another country. It is analogous to walking around a single gem, describing first this facet, then the other. But it is really only one gem. I can't guess at the precise hues in your facet. So I ask for your patience as you walk around with me. I am anxious that you enjoy the gem too. The only really satisfactory answer to all questions is the experience of the center. When asked some great cosmic question, the Buddha often fell silent. It was similar to saying, "No words of mine can bring you back to your center. Notice the birds singing. Enjoy the lovely clouds. Find your way back to the place of No-Question-Left." These experiences are not ever intellectual objects you can cleverly manipulate. And ultimately, it is as Buddha said, "Vigorously seek to find your own way."

Our circumambulation of the gem began with "An Introduction to Mysticism." There I hoped to set the general parameters and to answer some obvious questions. We are dealing with an experience that is said to be ineffable (beyond words), but somehow even in the mood of the words and how they are put together, the central experience is implied. The message is also in the medium, in the way it is expressed, hence poetry.

In the "Experience of God," I tried to be more specific about the marks of the experience. Basically, it is like having the whole of existence open like a flower showing itself. It is much too wonderful to mistake it for any of the little things you can do in your self. One mystic said it is like being shown everything at once. Yes, of course, that is what it is like.

The poem "In Appreciation" suggested that all the answers you could desire are in appreciating exactly what you already have. You have Awareness. Do you even really know what it is? Have you ever simply felt thankful for having what much of the cosmos doesn't have, this awareness? Though it may not have been clearly said, appreciation is characteristic of the mystical experience.

"Religion: A Human Enterprise" is an antidote to high-flown ideas. Look at religion as a human creation. Ask how it functions for people, and you see much of its heart. Religions vary widely from churches where there is much singing, fellowship, and free expression to religions of quiet monks and nuns reading the Psalms reflectively. This great variety gives people many choices. Religion as a human enterprise verges on the social sciences. Religions as human institutions make good sense. Picture one religion dominant, and all people had to be strained through its one form. Wouldn't it do much harm? We are varied enough to find different forms that suit us better. If this nondoctrinal social approach interests you, see the fine work of William Paden.[2] The field of comparative religion appreciates religions as human enterprises that make social sense. Comparative religion avoids disputes over differences. Like anthropologists, it just tries to understand human institutions.

"The Mystic's View of Salvation" was an attempt to nail down the central truth. In some ways, you are damned to a life of needless fear and strife if you conclude you are a lone ship on dangerous seas. Salvation rests upon discovering that the More-than-Self can be met, can be dealt with, and is the source of your very life. We are on a wise sea that launched us to specific ends, a sea deeply involved in our voyage.

The poem "Subtle Understanding" is a centerpiece. The intuition of a mystic is in subtle understanding. Gaze on a stream for an hour and look at the subtle understanding flowing along. The plant growing happily in its spot is in a subtle understanding of soil, air, sun, and seasons. The animal or human mother who lovingly cares for offspring is in subtle understanding. The mystic Swedenborg said that love conjoins, and there is understanding in what is conjoined. What you live with, you come to understand.

The "Way of Beauty" was an attempt to broaden the understanding of what is involved. Some would say "right" doctrine (that is, orthodox doctrine) leads into understanding one's relationship to God, and one cannot be involved in these things

---

2. William Paden, *Interpreting the Sacred* (Boston: Beacon Press, 1992); and *Religious Worlds* (Boston: Beacon Press, 1984). See also Huston Smith, *The Illustrated World's Religions* (San Francisco: Harper, 1994).

without predicating a God. This attitude puts many people outside of the mystical equation. In the first place, doctrine does not lead to an understanding of God; it only seems to. Real understanding of God comes only from a lifetime of interaction with God. If you were God, would you mind if someone lovingly interacted with you as Beauty? I think not. Wouldn't you delightfully speak the language of beauty to your subject? And if we can admit beauty, can't we admit all sorts of respectful interactions? Suppose a determined nonbeliever spent a lifetime in caring for unwanted children. Even according to Christ's saying, this one had been interacting with Christ all along, no matter what he or she chooses to call it. Thus, the mystical equation opens out to all loving, respectful interactions. We are dealing with a single broad process. Instead of "God," I have referred to dealing with the "More-than-Self," which can be given any name or no name. I am guided in this by a very close look at Swedenborg's *Heaven and Hell.* The turning point between hell and heaven is the difference between regarding yourself over all the rest of creation versus honoring any More-than-Self.

"Gazing at the Spiritual in an Icon" was chance to look into spiritual practice to see what occurs in it. All spiritual practices involve a simple, limited approach to the All. They have at their heart an attempt to shut off (or at least limit) ego in a naked encounter with the More-than-Self. Those outside spiritual practice of any kind might think it would be dull and boring. It is the exact opposite, full of life. It was an immense relief to find myself in the hands of a wisdom greater than mine. It was cheering to be led back into the traditions of millions who came before me. Dull? Some of the greatest experiences of my life came from gazing at my thirty-cent icon.[3]

---

3. I know of no really good compendium of practices from the viewpoint of a mystic. But here are a few accounts I would recommend: Romano Guardini, *The Art of Praying* (Manchester, N.H.: Sophia Institute, 1985); Madam Guyon, *Experiencing God through Prayer* (New Kensington, Penna.: Whitaker House,1984); Brother Lawrence, *The Practice of the Presence of God* (New York: Doubleday, 1977); and An Anonymous Pilgrim, *The Way of a Pilgrim* (Pasadena, Calif.: Hope Publishing House, 1993). This last is on the *Jesus Prayer,* the Western equivalent of the Eastern mantra.

My tour through the landscape of world mysticism crept up on me. After years of slowly collecting and enjoying the works of other mystics, it occurred to me that I needed to make sure I had seen it all. There was some trepidation. Would there be mystics I could not understand? Not really. The Eastern mystics were easier than the Western mystics to understand. I was rather slow to come to mystical Christianity, in part because it is mixed with so many other things. I had a long enjoyable tour through the Eastern Orthodox mystics. I spent so much time with Russian saints that I began to feel like a monk in the forests of Siberia, a friend of bears like the blessed St. Seraphim of Sarov. Another fear was that a serious study would show mystics were not in real agreement. There is an apparent East-West difference on reincarnation and lives beyond this one; but even this dichotomy was resolved for me.[4] It takes careful study to find there is no real difference between East and West. I was disappointed to find so little concerning pagan religions and that of indigenous peoples. What I found were not differences in essential discoveries but cultural differences. The different cultures ascend the mountain by different paths, but it is the same mountain. I came to appreciate that some mystics had simply gone further, and here I would name Emanuel Swedenborg in the West and the Mahayana Buddhists in the East. I was pleased to see the Golden Rule in so many different contexts. And I also found the essential doctrine that only God really exists enunciated in different ways by widely separated religions. So, though there are some cultural differences, the world's mystics have encountered the same One.

Our circumambulation around a giant gem has brought out various colors. Yet, if we stand back, we see not individual facets, but a single brilliant gem, a whole that contains each part and in

---

4. W. Van Dusen, "Reincarnation: The Universal Return," *Chrysalis* 11, no 3 (1987): 219–228; reprinted in *The County of Spirit*, 37–48 (San Francisco: J. Appleseed, 1992). Many understand that the little self returns, and this is promoted by the more casual Eastern and Western literature. But a careful study of great Eastern authorities indicates the little self is an illusion. The Universal, of course, returns endlessly. Without this, creation would end. There are a number of paradoxes in a thorough understanding of reincarnation.

which each part contributes. Let me end on the theme of the single order that includes all things, including ourselves.

The Universal Order

We have been circumambulating a gem. Another way to conceive of this gem is as the very order of existence. Suppose the whole of existence were in a given order. Wouldn't it be wise to come into harmony with this order?

In the material world, science has been most successful in working out details of the natural order. The ancient ones knew electricity as lightning. But science has worked out how to harness and use electricity and the related radio waves. Out of this, we have computers and countless electrical and electronic devices. We are working in harmony with the electrical potential of existence.

If you want a sense of the order and size of the universe, do not overlook the findings coming out of astronomy. Some would suppose a conflict between mysticism and science, but it is not so. All ways to discover the order of things are useful. Before science, we had philosophical speculation that led to conflicting arguments. Will a heavier ball fall faster than a lighter one? Well, let's climb a tower and drop them and see. Let us settle things with actual tests.

It is unfortunate that psychology and the social sciences are having a more difficult task of reaching certainty. But the methods of approach and statistics itself are improving. The methods of science are not yet applicable to mysticism. Certain less important matters could be approached by the social sciences, such as the differences in personalities in different faiths. But the central matters of mysticism are as yet beyond the scope of science, which is designed for observable matter. Yet, if you look across methods of spiritual practice, there is an underlying similarity to the practices that lead into spiritual experience. The mystics are like explorers who come back from distant lands to report as well as they can what they found. Swedenborg explored both heaven and hell and reported on what he found. He wondered if he dared to give actual accounts of his personal experience. The Lord assured him it was desirable, so here and there he reports memorable experiences. He was in hell dealing with what he knew to be a pretentious and deceptive spirit. I will let Swedenborg set the scene.

> *While I was gazing in wonder at all this, there suddenly emerged from the lower earth, where the disturbance was, a spirit who could take upon himself the appearance of an angel of light. "Where is the man," he shouted, "who talks and writes about an order, to which almighty God has restricted Himself in His dealings with man? News of this has penetrated the roof and reached us down below."*
>
> *When he came to the ground level, he hurried along a paved road; and eventually he came up to me and at once pretended to be an angel from heaven. Then, speaking in an assumed tone of voice, "Are you," he said, "the man who thinks and speaks about order? Give me a brief account of order and some examples of it."*

Notice that the spirit came from the lower earth and he speaks in an assumed tone of voice. Swedenborg gives him a remarkable answer that reflects much thought and experience. He is giving the essence of the universal order and how we are to live with it.

> *"I will give you," I replied, "a summary, but not the details, because these would be beyond your grasp." I told him: (i) God is Order itself. (ii) He created man from order according to order and to be subject to order. (iii) He created his rational mind in accordance with the order of the whole spiritual world and his body in accordance with the order of the whole natural world, which is why the ancients called man a micro-heaven and a microcosm. (iv) It is therefore a law of order that man from his micro-heaven or little spiritual world should control his microcosm or little natural world,*

*just as God from His macro-heaven or spiritual world con-
trols the macrocosm or natural world in all its parts. (v) A
consequential law of order is therefore that a person ought to
enter into faith by means of truths from the Word, and into
charity by means of good deeds, and so reform and regenerate himself. (vi) It is a law of order that a person should by
his own efforts and ability cleanse himself from sins, and not
stand idly confident of his inability to act, waiting for God to
wipe away his sins in an instant. (vii) It is also a law of order
that a person should love God with all his soul and all his
heart, and his neighbor as himself, and not hang back waiting for God instantaneously to place either love in his mind
and heart, like bread from the baker's in the mouth. I told
him much more besides.[5]*

This is a marvelous summary. Swedenborg begins with the
first essential. God is Order itself. Out of this arises all other aspects of order. He created the human from order, according to
order and to be subject to order. Ultimately, what we call ourselves
is just a bit of this common order. Hence, we are in all aspects
from order, made in accord with order, and subject to order.

Next, Swedenborg goes into how we are to live and respond in
view of this. He reveals an amazing aspect of his findings of
heaven and hell. God created the human's rational mind in accor-
dance with the order of the whole spiritual world. Hence, one of
the confirmations of Swedenborg's description of heaven and hell
is our own internal order, for we really are a microcosm that reflects the macrocosm of all there is. And our body is material and
reflects the order of the whole natural world. So, putting these together, we are each the conjoining of the spiritual to the natural.
Therefore, in terms of our responsibility, we are like a miniature
god of a little universe. The spiritual side of ourselves is super-
ordinate to our natural or bodily side.

---

5. Emanuel Swedenborg, *True Christian Religion*, trans. John C. Ager, 2 volumes, second edition
(West Chester, Penna.: Swedenborg Foundation, 1997), paragraph 71.

But, as little gods, how should we proceed? Let me repeat the answer: "It is therefore a law of order that man from his micro-heaven or little spiritual world should control his microcosm or little natural world, just as God does from His macro-heaven or spiritual world in all its parts. A consequent law of order is there-fore that a person ought to enter into faith by means of truths from the Word, and into charity by means of good deeds, and so reform and regenerate himself."

Swedenborg always links our understanding of truth to good deeds. Our understanding is no deeper or better than what we ac-tually try to do. Understanding here goes far beyond simply know-ing words. What we *do* is the very life and substance of our understanding, therefore, the true way to regenerate or reform ourselves. There is the implication that this is a lifelong process and even beyond—going from revealed truth to action, with our deeds being the actual substance and reality of our understanding.

In the last line, Swedenborg reemphasizes that the person is to try. I have often thought of our trying, or what he calls our real ends, as the real substance of the spiritual, not what one accom-plishes in a worldly sense. "It is a law of order that a person should by his own efforts and ability cleanse himself from sins, and not stand idly confident of his inability to act, waiting for God to wipe away his sins in an instant." Clearly, this passage emphasizes our effort. He restates what is the essence of Christianity and most re-ligions: "It is also a law or order that a person should love God with all his soul and all his heart and his neighbour as himself."

In another place, Swedenborg states the essence of human ef-fort in a more paradoxical way. We are to do our best while know-ing that whatever good comes out of this comes from God. God is the real source of our effort. If good comes of it, the Lord was there assisting us. Our good will takes place within God's will.

We can turn Swedenborg's statement on order into a useful spiritual practice. Let us reflect upon ourselves as *from* order and *in* order. We are an actual part of the order itself. But what kind of part? Is it like being a little wheel in a watch that blindly turns and, in turn, affects others? No. A key element in our being a part is that we are aware. Moreover, we can choose to cooperate with the order in which we are or fight order itself, spoiling the work of the watch. This makes us essentially different from a mechanical part. We are aware and can be a cooperative part.

The order we are in includes not only the whole outer created universe, but ourselves, our own innermost being. In *Heaven and Hell*, Swedenborg makes quite clear that the whole design of heaven and hell reflects in our inward mental and spiritual design. He is quite serious when he says we are a microcosm that reflects the design of the whole. Inwardly our order extends beyond our limited notions of ourselves. In effect, the mystery of the total order is both within us and outside of us. We meet the total order within and without, on all sides, everywhere.

How can these reasonable insights be turned into a spiritual practice? As an aware part of the whole, simply reflect on how all this is true. Reflect on this as you go through daily activities. For instance, in a garden reflect on how you bring order to the plants who are themselves in an order and how a handsome garden affects you internally. Or, in a store making a purchase, reflect on how this affects the salesperson who has a family to support. The Buddhist doctrine of interdependence is important. Frequently reflect on how you are in an order and are a part of the whole order. Do this as though you are discovering the universal order from your part in it.

This simple spiritual practice has a number of immediate benefits. A major one is that it tends to overcome egotism (what Swedenborg calls *proprium* or being for oneself alone). If you are reflecting on order, it is immediately apparent you are just a little bit of order. All the people, things, and activities around you are the larger order. You cannot get too presumptuous as just a bit of the whole.

There is another implication. If you are reflecting on order, you are open to discovering more about your relationship to all there is. This reflection brings a gradually deepening meaning both of your relationship to yourself and to the rest of existence. You will see yourself in the context of being dependent upon others and how you affect them.

There is a remarkable effect of this practice. Because you actually are in this order and reflecting on this order, the order gradually opens and reveals itself. Even the experience of heaven while in this life is possible. This practice is a fitting way to open order and discover more of it. And the more you are shown the easier it is to return to this simple practice. The experience of God is a preview to heaven.

Part of this spiritual practice is to reflect on your relationship to the depths of your being. Healing is one of the possibilities of this way. Self-discovery also equips you to relate in a wiser way to the total order. Ultimately, self-discovery and the appreciation of the total order in which you are embedded are the same things. Does this puzzle you? You—and all of us—are of the total order. Discovering yourself and the total order are the same thing. Or to put it in another way, you are from order, in order, and for order. Your choosing to learn and cooperate with order is a part of order arising to consciousness of itself. Become accustomed to the idea that, by your attempt to learn and cooperate, you become a knowing aspect of order itself. This practice gradually removes artificial conceptual boundaries.

There is another aspect to this practice. In the chapter "Way of Beauty," I attempted to broaden the narrowly conceived limits to other ways of human experience. Reflection on order does this too. An agnostic who has no confidence any God exists can easily see order and open him- or herself to a wider experience of order. Religious labels do not cover all of existence.

Give order any name you choose, as long as you are a part of this all. Order will not mind. Order customarily works within your viewpoint.

The more order is discovered the more perfect its design is found to be. It is a most amazing design. Indeed, it is very good, as the ancients said.

The respect for order arises naturally with a widening acquaintance with it. How much is there to learn this way? This learning is, thankfully, endless. What has been called enlightenment is just a temporary platform in an endless process.

Another way to describe mystical experience is entering the order of things.

Bibliography

Al-Din Rumi, Jalal. *The Essential Rumi*. Trans. Coleman Barks. San Francisco: Harper San Francisco, 1997.

Anonymous. *Splendour in the Night*. Kila, Mont.: Vessinger, 1993.

Anonymous Pilgrim, An. *The Way of a Pilgrim*. Pasadena, Calif.: Hope Publishing House, 1993.

Baggley, John. *Doors of Perception*. Crestwood, New York: St. Vladamir's Seminary Press, 1988.

Balsekar, Rames S. *The Final Truth*. Los Angeles: Advaita.

———. *Ripples*. Bombay, India.: Zen Publications, n.d.

Beck, Charlotte Joko. *Nothing Special*. San Francisco: Harper, 1993.

Beckett, Sister Wendy. *Meditations on Silence*. New York: Dorling Kindersley, 1995.

Bhave, Vinoba. *The Intimate and the Ultimate*. Longmead, England: Element, 1968.

Blofeld, John. *The Tantric Mysticism of Tibet*. New York: Dutton, 1970.

Bokar Rinpoche. *Death and the Art of Dying*. San Francisco: Clear Point Press, 1993.

Brother Lawrence. *The Practice of the Presence of God*. New York: Doubleday, 1977.

Buber, Martin. *Tales of the Hasidim.* New York: Schocken, 1991.

Ch'an, Chu, trans. *The Huang Po Doctrine of Universal Mind.* London: Buddhist Society, 1947.

Davis, Avram. *The Way of the Flame.* San Francisco: Harper, 1996.

De Caussade, Jean-Pierre. *Abandonment to Divine Providence.* New York: Doubleday, 1975.

De Project, Yeshe, ed. *The Art of Enlightenment.* Berkeley, Calif.: Dharma Publishing, 1985.

Dole, George F., and Robert H. Kirven. *A Scientist Explores Spirit.* Second edition. West Chester, Penna.: Chrysalis Books, 1997.

Easwaran, Eknath. *Gandhi the Man.* Petaluma, Calif.: Nilgiri Press, 1978.

Govinda, Lama Angarika. *Foundations of Tibetan Mysticism.* York Beach, Maine: 1969.

Gray, Lewis Fraley. *Speaks My Soul.* Sparks, Nev.: Box 2010, 1994.

Guardini, Romano. *The Art of Praying.* Manchester, New Hampshire: Sophia Institute, 1985.

Head, J., and S. L. Cranston. *Reincarnation: An East–West Anthology.* Wheaton, Ill.: Theosophical Publishing House, 1961.

Heschel, Abraham, *Man Is Not Alone.* New York: Noonday Press, 1951.

———. *The Prophets.* 2 vols. New York: Harper & Row, 1962.

Hua, Dhyana Master Hsuan. *A Several Explanation of the Vajra Prajna Paramita Sutra.* San Francisco: Buddhist Text Translation Society, 1974.

Hua, Master. *The Heart Sutra and Commentary.* San Francisco: Buddhist Text Translation Society, 1980.

Idel, Moshe. *Kabbalah.* New Haven, Conn.: Yale University Press, 1988.

James, William. *The Varieties of Religious Experience.* New York: Modern Library, 1902.

Kabir. *The Kabir Book: Forty-Four of the Ecstatic Poems of Kabir.* Edited by Robert Bly. Boston: Beacon Press, 1977; rpt. 1993.

Kalokyris, Constantine. *Orthodox Iconography.* Brookline, Mass.: Holy Cross Orthodox Press, 1985.

Khan, Pir Vilayat. *Introducing Spirituality into Counseling and Therapy.* New Lebanon, New York: Omega, 1982.

————. *Samadhi with Open Eyes.* New Lebanon, New York: Sufi Order, 1978.

Kongtrul, Jamgon. *The Great Path of Awakening.* Boston: Shambhala, 1987.

Longchenpa. *Kindly Bent to Ease Us.* 3 vols. Berkeley, Calif.: Dharma, 1976.

Madam Guyon. *Experiencing God through Prayer.* New Kensington, Penna.: Whitaker House, 1984.

Merton, Thomas. *The Way of Chuang Tzu.* Berkeley, Calif.: Shambhala, 1992.

Moses, Jeffrey. *Oneness.* New York: Fawcett, 1989.

Mother Meera. *Answer.* Ithaca, New York: Meeramma, 1991.

Naranjo, C., and R. Ornstein. *On the Psychology of Meditation.* New York: Viking, 1971.

Nasr, Seyyed. *Science and Civilization in Islam.* New York: Barnes and Noble, 1968.

Nicholson, Reynold A. *The Mystics of Islam.* London: Arkana, 1975.

Nikhilananda, Swami. *The Upanishads.* New York: Harper, 1949.

Nikodimus and Markarios. *The Philokalia.* 4 vols. Boston: Faber and Faber, 1979–1983.

Norbu, Namkhai. *Dzog Chen and Zen.* Nevada City, Calif.: Blue Dolphin Press, 1984.

Nouwen, Henri. *Behold the Lord.* Notre Dame, Ind.: Ave Maria Press, 1978.

Paden, William. *Interpreting the Sacred.* Boston: Beacon Press, 1992.

———. *Religious Worlds.* Boston: Beacon Press, 1984.

Plotinus. *The Essential Plotinus.* Trans. Elmer Green. New York: New American Library, 1964.

Ramana, Maharshi. *The Spiritual Teachings of Ramana Maharshi.* Boston: Shambhala, 1988.

Rogers, Carl, and Barry Stevens, eds. *Person to Person: The Problem of Being Human.* Walnut Creek, Calif.: Real People Press, 1967.

Sharma, Arvind. *Advaita Vedanta.* Delhi, India: Banarsidass, 1993.

Shraddhananda, Swami. *Seeing God Everywhere.* Hollywood, Calif.: Vedanta Press, 1996.

Smith, Huston. *The Illustrated World's Religions.* San Francisco: Harper, 1994.

Sogyal Rinpoche. *The Tibetan Book of Living and Dying.* San Francisco: Harper Collins, 1992.

Somé, Malidoma. *Of Water and the Spirit.* New York: Putnam's, 1994.

Spurgeon, C. F. E. *Mysticism in English Literature.* Kila, Mont.: Vessinger, 1913.

Stevens, John. *Three Zen Masters.* Tokyo: Kodansha, 1993.

Suzuki, D. T. *Mysticism: Christian and Buddhist.* New York: Collier, 1962.

_____. *Swedenborg: Buddha of the North.* Trans. Andrew Bernstein. West Chester, Penna.: Swedenborg Foundation, 1996.

_____. *The Zen Doctrine of No-Mind.* London: Rider, 1958.

Swedenborg, Emanuel. *Arcana Coelestia.* 12 vols. Trans. John F. Potts. Second edition. West Chester, Penna.: Swedenborg Foundation, 1995–1998.

_____. *Charity: The Practice of Neighborliness.* Trans. William F. Wunsch. Ed. William R. Woofenden. Second edition. West Chester, Penna.: Swedenborg Foundation, 1995.

_____. *Divine Love and Wisdom.* Trans. George F. Dole. West Chester, Penna.: Swedenborg Foundation, 1985,

_____. *Divine Love and Wisdom.* Trans. John C. Ager. Second edition. West Chester, Penna.: Swedenborg Foundation, 1996.

_____. *Divine Providence.* Trans. William Wunsch. Second edition. West Chester, Penna.: Swedenborg Foundation, 1996.

_____. *Heaven and Hell.* Trans. George F. Dole. West Chester, Penna.: Swedenborg Foundation, 1976.

_____. *Heaven and Its Wonders and Hell.* Trans. John C. Ager. Second edition. West Chester, Penna.: Swedenborg Foundation, 1995.

_____. *The Heavenly City: A Spiritual Guidebook.* Trans. Lee Woofenden. West Chester, Penna.: Swedenborg Foundation, 1993.

_____. *True Christian Religion.* 2 vols. Trans. John C. Ager. Second edition. West Chester, Penna.: Swedenborg Foundation, 1997.

Tagore, Rabindranath. *Gitanjali.* N.p., India: Macmillan, n.d.

————, trans. *Songs of Kabir.* York Beach, Maine: Weiser, 1991.

Theresa of Avila. *Interior Castle.* Garden City, New York: Double-day, 1961.

Toksvig, Signe. *Emanuel Swedenborg: Scientist and Mystic.* New York: Swedenborg Foundation, 1983.

Trobridge, George. *Swedenborg: Life and Teaching.* Rev. R. H. Tafel and R. H. Tafel Jr. New York: Swedenborg Foundation, 1992.

Tulku, Tarthang. *Sacred Art of Tibet.* Berkeley, Calif.: Dharma Publishing, 1974.

Turnbull, Grace H. *The Essence of Plotinus.* Kila, Mont.: Vessinger, 1934.

Underhill, Evelyn. *Mysticism.* New York: Dutton, 1961.

————. *Practical Mysticism.* New York: Dutton, 1915.

Van Dusen, Wilson. *The Country of Spirit: Selected Writings.* San Francisco: J. Appleseed & Co., 1992.

————. *The Natural Depth in Man.* New York: Swedenborg Foundation, 1981.

————. *The Presence of Other Worlds.* West Chester, Penna.: Swedenborg Foundation, 1991.

————. *Returning to the Source.* Moab, Utah: Real People Press, 1996.

Walshe, M. O'C. *Meister Eckhart.* 3 vols. Boston: Element, 1987.

Wilkinson, J. J. G., trans. *Swedenborg's Journal of Dreams, 1743–1744.* With commentary by Wilson Van Dusen. New York: Swedenborg Foundation, 1986.

Yeshe, Lama. *Introduction to Tantra.* Boston: Wisdom: Publications, 1987.

About the Author

Wilson Van Dusen was born and raised in San Francisco, California. Both of his parents were averse to religion; in spite of this, he came into the direct experience of God, even when he was an infant. In this family, he hid this interest. By adolescence, he quietly and systematically explored what opened mystical experience.

Van Dusen always wanted to be a naval officer; and in World War II, he became an officer in both the Merchant Marine and the Naval Reserve. At the end of the war, he dashed through academic degrees, ending with a Ph.D. in clinical psychology. He spent years with schizophrenics, with his most famous paper linking their hallucinatory experience to what the mystic Emanuel Swedenborg describes of hell. As a psychologist, he gravitated toward the direct description of the depths of human experience, with a special reference to the natural human potential for the experience of God.

Since his retirement, Van Dusen has spent fifteen years as a volunteer teacher of naval sciences to Coast Guard officers. He has studied mysticism across all religious lines and considers himself a representative of the universal of religion; he looks for the spiritual universal that transcends cultural and doctrinal differences. In his late years, his life has focused on presenting this concept in his writings.

Wilson Van Dusen is a frequent contributor to the Chrysalis Reader series, published by the Swedenborg Foundation. He is the author of numerous works, including *The Natural Depth in Man, The Presence of Other Worlds: The Psychological/Spiritual Findings of Emanuel Swedenborg, Country of Spirit,* and *Returning to the Source: The Way to the Experience of God.*

THE PRESENCE OF OTHER WORLDS
THE PSYCHOLOGICAL/ SPIRITUAL FINDINGS OF EMANUEL SWEDENBORG
Wilson Van Dusen

"An exciting and thought-provoking book which will appeal...to those persons who are not afraid of the inner psychic world." —*Carl Rogers*

An account of Swedenborg's journey through the "dark recesses of the psyche toward the Divine," an account that Van Dusen explains and clarifies through the lens of modern psychology and spiritual study.

0-87785-247-2, pb, $11.95

NATURAL DEPTH IN MAN
Wilson Van Dusen

A clinical psychologist draws from personal experience, work with mental patients, and Eastern and Western philosophy to guide the reader through the secret spaces of the inner world. Brief summaries at end of chapters help the reader distill meaning.

0-87785-165-4, pb, $8.95

LIGHT IN MY DARKNESS
Helen Keller; Edited by Ray Silverman

"...an inspiring picture of this remarkable woman's affirmation of the power and triumph of the spirit."
—*New Age Retailer*

Helen Keller's optimism and service to humanity were inspired by her readings of Swedenborg, whose insights she called her "strongest incitement to overcome limitations." This is Keller's 1927 spiritual autobiography, revised and enlarged with her letters, speeches, and other writings.

0-87785-146-8, pb, photos, $12.95

ANGELS IN ACTION
WHAT SWEDENBORG SAW AND HEARD
Robert H. Kirven

"Kirven presents Swedenborg's ideas and defends and promotes them in modern terms." —*Booklist*

For the last twenty-seven years of his life, Emanuel Swedenborg visited heaven and hell almost daily, meeting angels and evil spirits. His visions and their meanings are explained in this remarkable book. Kirven shows how angels work for us from birth through death and how we can be angels on earth.

0-87785-147-6, pb, illus., $11.95

A SCIENTIST EXPLORES SPIRIT
A BIOGRAPHY OF EMANUEL SWEDENBORG, WITH KEY CONCEPTS OF HIS THEOLOGY
George F. Dole and Robert H. Kirven

"Swedenborg is like a whole Himalayan Range of the mind. This biography, ...as from a mountain top, presents the whole vista of wisdom."
Wilson Van Dusen

This lively, concise revision introduces the life and spiritual thought of Emanuel Swedenborg. Of interest is the tension between science and spirit, and their ultimate confluence in Swedenborg's life and work.

0-87785-241-3, pb, illus., $10.95

HIDDEN MILLENNIUM
THE DOOMSDAY FALLACY
Stephen Koke
Foreword by David Spangler

"A balanced, concise, well-documented account of speculation and concern about the millennium.... Quite an absorbing book." —*Booklist*

Summarizing traditional millennial movements, *Hidden Millennium* explains why past doomsday prophesies have failed to materialize. Dire predictions contrast with the symbolic interpretation offered by Emanuel Swedenborg, who sees the Last Judgment as personal, not worldly, and hopeful, not fearful.

0-87785-376-2, pb, $14.95

DECISIONS! DECISIONS!
THE DYNAMICS OF CHOICE
Carol S. Lawson
& Robert F. Lawson, Editors
Foreword by Susan Cheever

This illustrated collection of original stories, poems, and essays broadens and brightens our pathways of possibilities. The richness and clarity of reflection show that the care taken to understand the context and the intent of decision are as important as the "yea" or "nay" of the choice itself.

0-87785-230-8, pb, 160 pp, illus., $13.95,
SIXTH CHRYSALIS READER

HEAVEN & HELL
Emanuel Swedenborg
Translated by George F. Dole

"One of the most fascinating guides to other worlds in the Western spiritual canon." —*Gary Lachman, Gnosis*

First published in 1758, *Heaven and Hell* fully describes the life hereafter. Dole's easy-to-read translation makes Swedenborg's experiences accessible to all. Swedenborg describes heaven, the world of spirits, and hell, and explains their meaning and relationship to our lives in the earthly realm.

0-87785-153-0, pb, $12.95

VIDEOTAPES

SWEDENBORG
THE MAN WHO HAD TO KNOW
with Lillian Gish; Eddie Albert, narrator.

Televised over 2,500 times, this film presents one of history's most fascinating personalities, Emanuel Swedenborg, and depicts his visionary insights.

VHS, 30 min, $29.95

JOHNNY APPLESEED
AND THE FRONTIER WITHIN
with Lillian Gish.

The true story of American folk hero Johnny "Appleseed" Chapman, frontier mystic and self-appointed Swedenborgian minister. Cross the ultimate threshold.

VHS, 30 min, $29.95

Available at bookstores, or:

Individuals:
Call **800-355-3222**
or order through our secured
web site at **www.swedenborg.com**

or write:
Swedenborg Foundation Publishers
320 North Church Street
West Chester, PA 19380

Booksellers:
Call Words Distributing Company
800-593-WORD (9673)